Harrison

SPECTRUM®

Algebra

Grades 6–8

Published by Spectrum®
an imprint of Carson-Dellosa Publishing LLC
Greensboro, NC

Spectrum® is an imprint of Carson-Dellosa Publishing.

Send all inquiries to:
Carson-Dellosa Publishing
P.O. Box 35665
Greensboro, NC 27425 USA

Printed in the USA

ISBN 978-0-7696-6306-7

04-214127811

Table of Contents Algebra

Table of Contents, continued

Chapter 9 Algebra and Geometry

NAME ____________________

CHAPTER 1 PRETEST

Check What You Know

Algebra Basics

Identify each of the following as an expression, an equation, or an inequality.

	a	b
1.	$x - 3$ ________	$3 + b > 9$ ________
2.	$4 + 3 = 7$ ________	$32 - 8$ ________

Identify each of the following as a numerical expression or a variable expression.

3.	$10 \div 2$ ________	$10 - n$ ________
4.	$2b + 4$ ________	8×12 ________

Write each phrase as an algebraic expression. Use n for an unknown number.

5.	three less than x ________	a number divided by seven ________
6.	the product of 10 and 9 ________	five more than a ________

Write each sentence as an equation or inequality. Use n for an unknown number.

7.	The product of 3 and n is 12. ________	Five less than n is seven. ________
8.	Two more than n is less than 10. ________	Eighteen divided by n is six. ________

Write each of the following expressions or equations in words.

9.	$7 + n$	$3n + 2 = 29$
	____________________	____________________

Name the property shown by each statement.

10.	$0 \times 9 = 0$ ________	$23 \times 1 = 23$ ________
11.	$3 \times 6 = 6 \times 3$ ________	$5 \times (8 \times 2) = (5 \times 8) \times 2$ ________

NAME ___________________________

Check What You Know

Algebra Basics

Complete or rewrite each equation using the property indicated.

	a	b
12.	Commutative: 9 + 8 = ________	Associative: 5 × (3 × 4) = ________
13.	Identity: 91 + 0 = ________	Property of Zero: 72 × 0 = ________

Underline the operation that should be completed first.

14.	(6 + 1) × 4	3 × 4 ÷ 3 − 2
15.	88 − 5 × 8	(12 ÷ 3) − (2 × 2)
16.	22 − 2 + 3	5 − 2 × 4

Find the value of each expression.

17.	(3 + 4) × (6 + 1) ________	3 + 2 × 3 + 4 ________
18.	(5 × 3) + (4 × 7) ________	(3 + 2) × (3 + 4) ________
19.	12 − (2 + 5) ________	12 − 2 + 5 ________

Write the ordered pair for each lettered point on Grid I.

20. *A* ________ *B* ________

21. *C* ________ *D* ________

Plot each of the following ordered pairs on Grid I.

22. *E* (7, 7) *F* (−2, −5)

G (−4, 3) *H* (4, −6)

Grid I

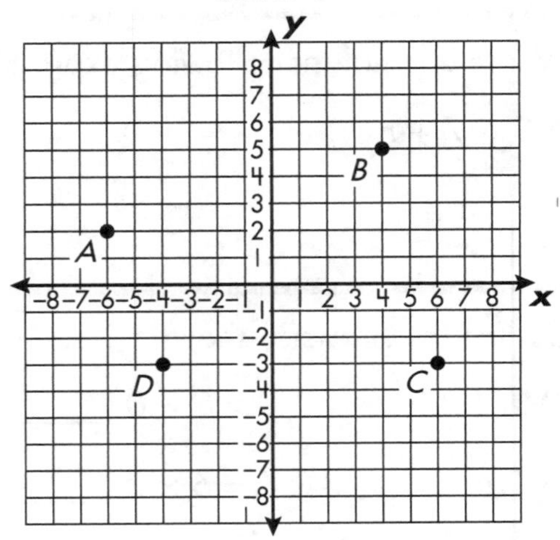

NAME ______________________

Lesson 1.1 Expressions and Variables

An **expression** is a number phrase without an equals sign. A **variable** is a symbol, usually a letter, that stands for an unknown number or quantity.

An **algebraic expression** is a number, variable, or combination of numbers and variables, connected by a mathematical operation like addition, subtraction, multiplication, or division. For example, in the expression $x + 5$, x is the variable.

A **numerical expression** contains only numbers: $3 + 6$

A **variable expression** contains numbers and variables: $3 + b$

All expressions express an idea.

$5n$ means "five times n" or "five ns."
$b - 3$ means "b decreased by 3" or "a number decreased by 3."

Write whether each of the following is a numerical expression or a variable expression.

	a	b	c
1.	$s + 15$ ________	4×6 ________	$10 - r$ ________
2.	$55 - 23$ ________	21×3 ________	$b + 7$ ________

Translate each phrase into an algebraic expression.

	a	b
3.	a number increased by 2 ________	4 less than 11 ________
4.	the product of 9 and 8 ________	r added to 10 ________
5.	b divided by 5 ________	three 7s ________
6.	s decreased by 1 ________	6 more than 12 ________

Write the following expressions in words.

7. $d + 2$ ______________________________

8. $3 \times n$ ______________________________

NAME ____________________

Lesson 1.2 Properties

The **Commutative Properties of Addition and Multiplication** state that the order in which numbers are added or multiplied does not change the result.

$a + b = b + a$	and	$a \times b = b \times a$
$2 + 3 = 5$		$5 \times 2 = 10$
$3 + 2 = 5$		$2 \times 5 = 10$

The **Associative Properties of Addition and Multiplication** state that the way in which addends and factors are grouped does not change the result.

$(a + b) + c = a + (b + c)$	and	$(a \times b) \times c = a \times (b \times c)$
$(2 + 3) + 4 = 2 + (3 + 4)$		$(2 \times 4) \times 5 = 2 \times (4 \times 5)$
$5 + 4 = 2 + 7$		$8 \times 5 = 2 \times 20$
$9 = 9$		$40 = 40$

The **Identity Property of Addition** states that the sum of an addend and 0 is the addend.

$a + 0 = a$ $\quad$ $5 + 0 = 5$

The **Identity Property of Multiplication** states that the product of a factor and 1 is the factor.

$a \times 1 = a$ $\quad$ $4 \times 1 = 4$

The **Properties of Zero** state that the product of a factor and 0 is 0. They also state that the quotient of zero and any non-zero divisor is 0.

$a \times 0 = 0$ $\quad 5 \times 0 = 0$ $\quad$ and $\quad$ $0 \div a = 0$ $\quad 0 \div 5 = 0$

Name the property shown by each statement.

	a	b
1.	$63 \times 1 = 63$ ________	$0 \times b = 0$ ________
2.	$3 \times (5 \times 7) = (3 \times 5) \times 7$ ________	$91 + 0 = 91$ ________
3.	$9 \times 8 = 8 \times 9$ ________	$0 \div 2 = 0$ ________

Complete or rewrite each equation using the property indicated.

	a	b
4.	Identity: $0 + y =$ ________	Associative: $6 \times (7 \times 8) =$ ________
5.	Commutative: $5 + 4 =$ ________	Properties of Zero: $0 \times 10 =$ ________
6.	Associative: $7 + (b + 9) =$ ________	Commutative: $10 \times 3 =$ ________

NAME ______________________

Lesson 1.3 Equations and Inequalities

An **equation** is a mathematical sentence that states that two expressions are equal. It contains an equals sign.

$2 + 5 = 7$

An **inequality** is a mathematical sentence that states that two expressions are not equal. It shows how two numbers or expressions compare to one another.

$2 + 5 > 6$ $2 + 5 < 9$

Like expressions, equations and inequalities may contain only numerals, or they may also contain variables.

$2 + c = 7$

Write whether each of the following is an equation or an inequality.

	a	b
1.	$76 - 23 = 53$ ________	$x - 7 > 5$ ________
2.	$9 \times n < 80$ ________	$4 + s = 10$ ________

Translate each sentence into an equation or inequality. Use *n* for an unknown number.

3. Seven less than a number is five. ________

4. The product of nine and three is twenty-seven. ________

5. Five more than a number is less than 60. ________

6. Ten divided by *n* equals two. ________

Write each equation or inequality in words.

7. $x \div 3 = 12$ ______________________

8. $5 \times 21 > 100$ ______________________

9. $7n + 3 = 31$ ______________________

10. $29 - s < 10$ ______________________

NAME ______________________________

Lesson 1.4 Order of Operations

If an expression contains two or more operations, they must be completed in a specified order. The **order of operations** is as follows:

1. Do all operations within parentheses and/or brackets (innermost first).
2. Do all multiplications and divisions, in order from left to right.
3. Do all additions and subtractions, in order from left to right.

$3 \times (4 + 5) + 6 \div 3$	Do the operation within the parentheses first.
$3 \times 9 + 6 \div 3$	Multiply and divide from left to right.
$27 + 2$	Add.
29	

Underline the operation that should be performed first.

	a	b
1.	$30 - 5 \times 2$	$(10 \div 2) + (4 \times 2)$
2.	$2 \times 10 \div 5 - 1$	$3 \times 4 \times 6$
3.	$(8 + 2) \times 3$	$16 - 8 + 2$
4.	$52 - 10 \times 2 \div 5$	$5 \times [15 \div (11 - 8)]$

Find the value of each expression.

5.	$(8 - 3) \times 2$ ________	$8 - (3 \times 2)$ ________
6.	$10 - (5 + 2)$ ________	$10 - 5 + 2$ ________
7.	$(2 + 3) \times (4 + 5)$ ________	$2 + 3 \times 4 + 5$ ________
8.	$(9 \times 3) + (9 \times 2)$ ________	$[9 \times (6 - 3)] \times 2$ ________

Find the value of each expression if $a = 2$ and $b = 3$.

9.	$5a + 2 - 1$ ________	$(b + 6) \times 4$ ________
10.	$(4a + 3b) - 2$ ________	$(3a + 3) \div b$ ________

NAME ___________________________

Lesson 1.5 Coordinate Systems, Ordered Pairs, and Relations

A coordinate plane is formed by two intersecting number lines. The horizontal line is called the *x*-axis. The vertical line is called the *y*-axis. This two-axis system is called the **coordinate system.**

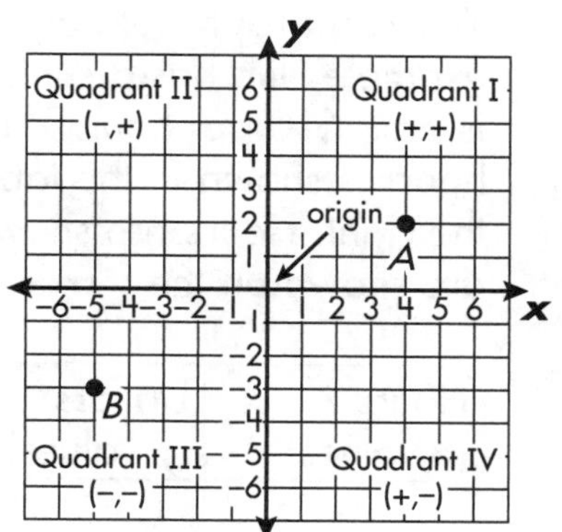

The coordinates of a point are represented by the ordered pair (*x*, *y*). This shows the distance the point is from the origin (0, 0), in the **domain** (the set of *x* coordinates) and the **range** (the set of *y* coordinates).

In the graph at right, Point *A* is located at (4, 2). Point *B* is located at (–5, –3).

A set of ordered pairs is called a **relation**.

Write the ordered pair for each lettered point on Grid I.

Grid 1

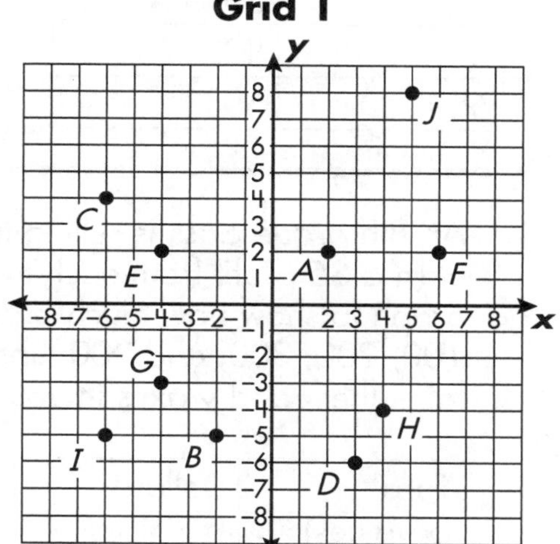

1. *A* ________ *B* ________
2. *C* ________ *D* ________
3. *E* ________ *F* ________
4. *G* ________ *H* ________
5. *I* ________ *J* ________

Plot each ordered pair below on Grid 2. Label the points.

Grid 2

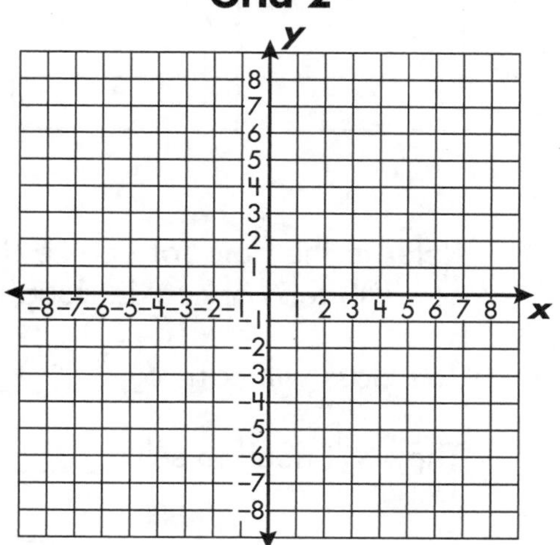

6. *A* (2, 1) *B* (2, –5)
   C (–2, –7) *D* (–6, 6)
   E (4, 6) *F* (3, –2)
   G (–4, –6) *H* (–7, 8)
   I (5, 8) *J* (–3, 2)

NAME ____________________

Lesson 1.5 Coordinate Systems, Ordered Pairs, and Relations

You can graph data using ordered pairs. For example, Jim has a summer job mowing lawns. He is paid $10 per hour. The amount he can earn in five hours is shown in the table below and in the graph to the right. Hours are shown on the *x*-axis, and dollars are shown on the *y*-axis.

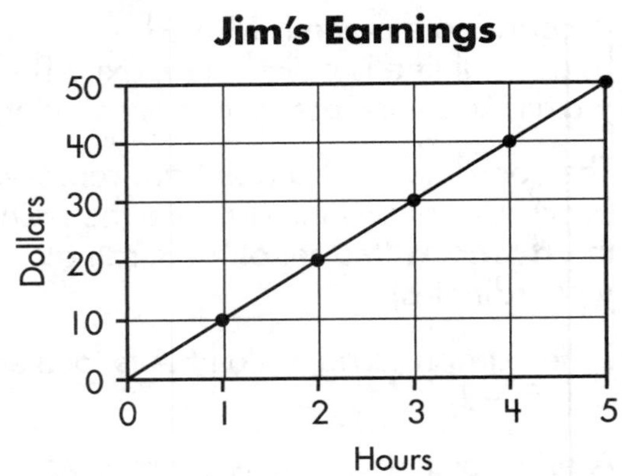

Hours (*x* values)	Dollars (*y* values)
1	10
2	20
3	30
4	40
5	50

1. An 8th-grade class is selling tubs of cookie dough. They earn a $5 profit from each tub sold. Make a table and graph to show how much profit they will earn if they sell 100, 200, 300, and 400 tubs of cookie dough. Be sure to label the *x* and *y* axes in your graph.

Profit from Cookie Dough Sales

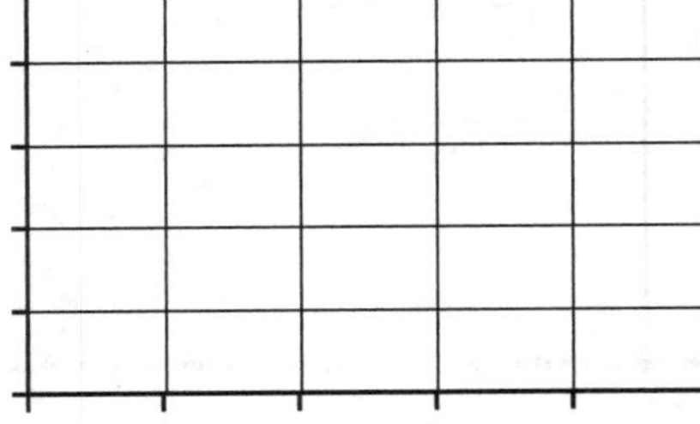

Tubs (*x* values)	Dollars (*y* values)

2. Refer to the data for cookie dough sales in problem 1. How much will the class earn if they sell 400 tubs of cookie dough? How many tubs will they need to sell to earn $3,000?

The class will earn $________.

They will need to sell ________ tubs.

NAME ____________________

Check What You Learned

Algebra Basics

Identify each of the following as an expression, an equation, or an inequality.

	a	b
1.	$n + 5 = 8$ ________	$71 - x$ ________
2.	$41 - 3$ ________	$10 + n < 35$ ________

Identify each of the following as a numerical expression or a variable expression.

3.	$3n - 2$ ________	7×11 ________
4.	$35 \div 7$ ________	$13 + b$ ________

Write each phrase as an algebraic expression. Use n for an unknown number.

5.	b divided by three ________	the product of seven and n ________
6.	ten less than 42 ________	seven decreased by n ________

Write each sentence as an equation. Use n for an unknown number.

7.	Seven decreased by three is four. ________	Twelve divided by a number is three. ________
8.	Six less than x is more than ten. ________	The product of 5 and b is 20. ________

Write each of the following expressions or equations in words.

9.	$b + 22$	$2b + 7 = 15$
	____________________	____________________

Name the property shown by each statement.

10.	$41 \times 1 = 41$ ________	$10 + 20 = 20 + 10$ ________
11.	$6 + (1 + 3) = (6 + 1) + 3$ ________	$11 \times 2 = 2 \times 11$ ________

CHAPTER 1 POSTTEST

NAME ____________________

Check What You Learned

Algebra Basics

Complete or rewrite each equation using the property indicated.

	a	b
12.	Property of Zero: $0 \div 33 =$ ________	Identity: $88 + 0 =$ ________
13.	Associative: $2 + (4 + 5) =$ ________	Commutative: $6 \times 8 =$ ________

Underline the operation that should be completed first.

14.	$8 - 3 \times 2$	$(4 + 3) \times 2$
15.	$12 \div 3 \times 2$	$37 - 4 + 6$
16.	$(3 \times 2) - (10 \div 5)$	$2 \times [12 \div (5 - 3)]$

Find the value of each expression.

17.	$(6 + 1) \times (5 - 3)$ ________	$6 + 1 \times 5 - 3$ ________
18.	$10 - 3 + 4$ ________	$10 - (3 + 4)$ ________
19.	$(2 \times 3) + (3 \times 4)$ ________	$3 \times [10 \div (4 - 2)]$ ________

Write the ordered pair for each lettered point on Grid I.

20. *A* ________ *B* ________

21. *C* ________ *D* ________

Plot each of the following ordered pairs on Grid I.

22. *E* (–3, –2) *F* (–5, 4)

G (6, –2) *H* (2, 7)

Grid I

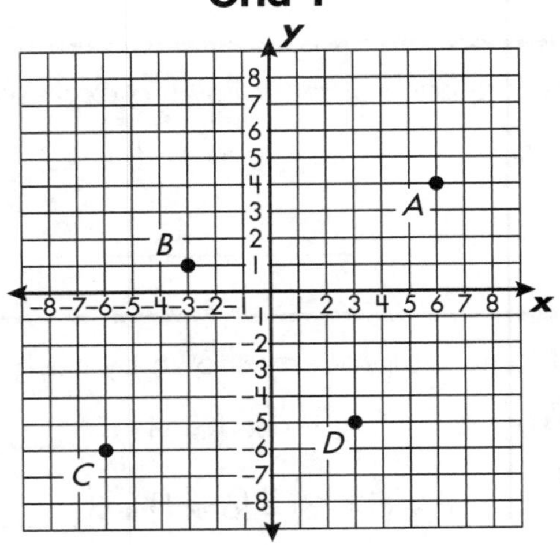

NAME ______________________

Check What You Know

Integers and Equations

Add or subtract.

	a	b	c	d
1.	$5 + 3 =$ ______	$-5 + (-3) =$ ______	$5 + (-3) =$ ______	$-5 + 3 =$ ______
2.	$5 - 3 =$ ______	$-5 - 3 =$ ______	$5 - (-3) =$ ______	$-5 - (-3) =$ ______

Multiply or divide.

3.	$2 \times 6 =$ ______	$-2 \times 6 =$ ______	$2 \times (-6) =$ ______	$-2 \times (-6) =$ ______
4.	$6 \div 2 =$ ______	$6 \div (-2) =$ ______	$-6 \div 2 =$ ______	$-6 \div -2 =$ ______
5.	$5 \div (-1) =$ ______	$-5 \times (-1) =$ ______	$5 \div (-5) =$ ______	$-5 \div (-5) =$ ______

Rewrite each expression using the Distributive Property.

	a	b
6.	$4 \times (6 + 7) =$ ____________	$(2 \times 3) + (2 \times 5) =$ ____________
7.	$6 \times (4 - 3) =$ ____________	$(4 \times 8) - (4 \times 9) =$ ____________

Simplify each algebraic expression.

8. $4(3a + 7) + 5(2a - 2)$ ______

9. $5(b + 9) - 7(4b - 3)$ ______

10. $6(4c - 3) + 2(2 - c)$ ______

NAME ______________________

Check What You Know

Integers and Equations

Solve each equation

	a	b	c
11.	$4 + s = 11$ ______	$t + 9 = 21$ ______	$16 = n + 12$ ______
12.	$27 - z = 4$ ______	$x - 13 = 42$ ______	$5 = 51 - b$ ______
13.	$c - 19 = 0$ ______	$r + 5 = 10$ ______	$1 = n - 10$ ______
14.	$3 \times s = 27$ ______	$t \times 9 = 81$ ______	$6a = 42$ ______
15.	$z \div 5 = 4$ ______	$72 \div c = 18$ ______	$\frac{b}{17} = 3$ ______
16.	$\frac{20}{t} = 4$ ______	$9 = \frac{x}{3}$ ______	$0 = 15d$ ______
17.	$5b + 3 = 13$ ______	$7p - 5 = 16$ ______	$\frac{r}{10} - 3 = 1$ ______

Write an equation for each problem. Then, solve the equation.

18. In Chase's art class, there are 21 students. Nine of them are girls. How many are boys?

______________ There are ________ boys in the class.

19. Garrett earns $8.00 an hour in his summer job. Each week, he earns $160. How many hours per week does he work?

______________ He works ________ hours per week.

20. Brenna bought a necklace for $10 and three bracelets. She spent a total of $28. If each bracelet cost the same amount, how much did each bracelet cost?

______________ Each bracelet cost ________ dollars.

NAME ______________________

Lesson 2.1 Adding and Subtracting Integers

Integers are the set of whole numbers and their opposites.

Positive integers are greater than zero. Negative integers are less than zero. A negative integer is less than a positive integer. The smaller of two integers is always the one to the left on the number line.

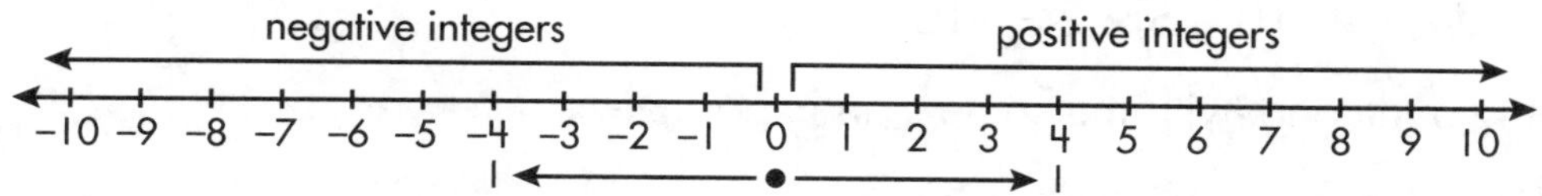

The opposite of 4 is −4. They are both 4 spaces from 0.

The sum of two positive integers is positive. The sum of two negative integers is negative.

Examples: 4 + 3 = 7 −4 + (−3) = −7

To find the sum of two integers with different signs, find their absolute values. Absolute value is the distance (in units) that a number is from 0 expressed as a positive quantity. Subtract the lesser number from the greater number. The sum has the same sign as the integer with the larger absolute value.

Example: −4 + 3 = − (4 − 3) = −1

To subtract an integer, add its opposite.

Example: 5 − 7 = 5 + (−7) = −2

Add or subtract.

	a	b	c	d
1.	2 + 4 = ______	−2 + (−4) = ______	2 + (−4) = ______	−2 + 4 = ______
2.	4 − 2 = ______	−4 − 2 = ______	4 − (−2) = ______	−4 − (−2) = ______
3.	−5 + (−5) = ______	5 + (−5) = ______	−5 + 5 = ______	5 + 5 = ______
4.	2 − 4 = ______	−2 − 4 = ______	2 − (−4) = ______	−2 − (−4) = ______
5.	6 + (−16) = ______	6 − 16 = ______	−6 − 16 = ______	−6 + 16 = ______
6.	−7 + 7 = ______	−7 + 0 = ______	−7 − (−7) = ______	−7 − 7 = ______

NAME ____________________

Lesson 2.2 Multiplying and Dividing Integers

The product of two integers with the same sign is positive.

Examples: $5 \times 2 = 10$ $\quad -5 \times -2 = 10$

The product of two integers with different signs is negative.

Examples: $5 \times (-2) = -10$ $\quad -5 \times 2 = -10$

The quotient of two integers with the same sign is positive.

Examples: $10 \div 2 = 5$ $\quad -10 \div -2 = 5$

The quotient of two integers with different signs is negative.

Examples: $10 \div (-2) = -5$ $\quad -10 \div 2 = -5$

Multiply or divide.

	a	b	c	d
1.	$4 \times 3 =$ ______	$-5 \times 7 =$ ______	$9 \times (-4) =$ ______	$-4 \times (-5) =$ ______
2.	$15 \div 5 =$ ______	$20 \div (-5) =$ ______	$-10 \div 2 =$ ______	$12 \div (-4) =$ ______
3.	$-9 \times 8 =$ ______	$7 \times (-6) =$ ______	$-4 \times (-9) =$ ______	$-5 \times 10 =$ ______
4.	$8 \div (-1) =$ ______	$-16 \div 4 =$ ______	$25 \div (-5) =$ ______	$32 \div 8 =$ ______
5.	$17 \times (-3) =$ ______	$-7 \times (-1) =$ ______	$9 \times (-12) =$ ______	$-8 \times (-9) =$ ______
6.	$72 \div (-4) =$ ______	$-56 \div 8 =$ ______	$-77 \div (-7) =$ ______	$16 \div 8 =$ ______
7.	$6 \times 9 =$ ______	$7 \times (-7) =$ ______	$-19 \times (-2) =$ ______	$-3 \times 3 =$ ______
8.	$27 \div (-9) =$ ______	$-42 \div 2 =$ ______	$-14 \div (-1) =$ ______	$-63 \div 9 =$ ______

NAME ______________________

Lesson 2.3 The Distributive Property

The **Distributive Property** combines the operations of addition and multiplication.

It states that: $a \times (b + c) = (a \times b) + (a \times c)$

$3 \times (2 + 5) = (3 \times 2) + (3 \times 5)$

$3 \times 7 = 6 + 15$

$21 = 21$

It also means that $a \times (b - c) = (a \times b) - (a \times c)$

The Distributive Property helps simplify algebraic expressions. To simplify an algebraic expression:

1. Remove parentheses, using the Distributive Property.
2. Combine like terms. A term is a number, variable, or the product of a number and variable(s) in an algebraic expression. In the expression $3a + 5$, $3a$ is a term, and 5 is also a term. Like terms have the same variables. For example, in the expression $1 + 2x + 3y + 4x + 5$, $2x$ and $4x$ are like terms.
3. Combine the constants. A constant is a term that contains only a number. For example, in the expression $1 + 2x + 3y + 4x + 5$, 1 and 5 are constants.

Example: Simplify $2(4x - 5) - 3(6x + 5)$.

$2(4x) - 2(5) - 3(6x) - 3(5)$

$8x - 10 - 18x - 15$

$-10x - 10 - 15$

$-10x - 25$

Rewrite each expression using the Distributive Property.

	a	b
1.	$5 \times (3 + 4) =$ ________	$(3 \times 4) + (3 \times 6) =$ ________
2.	$15 \times (7 - 4) =$ ________	$(6 \times 5) - (5 \times 7) =$ ________
3.	$11 \times (5 + b) =$ ________	$13(m - n) =$ ________

Simplify each algebraic expression.

4. $3(7a + 8) - 4(3a - 2)$ ________

5. $b(9 - 2) + 6(2 - b)$ ________

NAME ____________________

Lesson 2.4 Solving Addition and Subtraction Equations

The **Addition and Subtraction Properties of Equality** state that when the same number is added to both sides of an equation, the two sides remain equal:

$4 + 17 = 21$ $\quad$ $4 + 17 + 5 = 21 + 5$ $\quad$ $26 = 26$

When the same number is subtracted from both sides of an equation, the two sides remain equal:

$32 = 16 + 16$ $\quad$ $32 - 4 = 16 + 16 - 4$ $\quad$ $28 = 28$

Use these properties to solve equations.

$a + 3 = 14$	$b - 11 = 6$
$a + 3 - 3 = 14 - 3$	$b - 11 + 11 = 6 + 11$
$a = 11$	$b = 17$

Solve each equation.

	a	b	c
1.	$8 + m = 13$ ________	$q + 7 = 15$ ________	$13 + b = 24$ ________
2.	$21 - c = 2$ ________	$61 - s = 30$ ________	$x - 5 = 5$ ________
3.	$34 - z = 0$ ________	$n - 41 = 60$ ________	$b - 12 = 1$ ________
4.	$22 = 10 + b$ ________	$5 = 23 - p$ ________	$11 = n + 5$ ________

Write an equation for each problem. Then, solve the equation.

5. Alicia baked 6 batches of cookies. 2 batches were peanut butter, 1 batch was oatmeal, and the rest were chocolate chip. How many batches were chocolate chip?

____________________ Alicia baked ________ chocolate chip batches.

6. Austin has 15 CDs, which is 3 less than his sister has. How many CDs does his sister have?

____________________ His sister has ________ CDs.

NAME ______________________

Lesson 2.5 Solving Multiplication and Division Equations

The **Multiplication and Division Properties of Equality** state that when each side of the equation is multiplied by the same number, the two sides remain equal.

$3 + 4 = 7$ $(3 + 4) \times 5 = 7 \times 5$ $35 = 35$

When each side of the equation is divided by the same number, the two sides remain equal.

$2 \times 6 = 12$ $\frac{(2 \times 6)}{3} = \frac{12}{3}$ $4 = 4$

Use these properties to solve equations.

$3 \times n = 15$	$n \div 6 = 8$
$3 \times \frac{n}{3} = \frac{15}{3}$	$n \div 6 \times 6 = 8 \times 6$
$n = 5$	$n = 48$

Solve each equation.

	a	b	c
1.	$4 \times b = 12$ ________	$p \times 12 = 36$ ________	$7a = 35$ ________
2.	$m \div 11 = 2$ ________	$42 \div q = 6$ ________	$\frac{s}{13} = 2$ ________
3.	$\frac{100}{t} = 5$ ________	$0 = c \times 21$ ________	$49 = 7 \times d$ ________
4.	$3 = \frac{r}{4}$ ________	$\frac{9}{z} = 1$ ________	$4k = 120$ ________

Write an equation for each problem. Then, solve the equation.

5. Sabrina spent $6.25 for drinks for her friends. If each drink cost $1.25, how many drinks did she buy?

______________________ She bought ________ drinks.

6. Luis has 3 times as many comic books as his best friend Orlando. If Luis has 12 comic books, how many does Orlando have?

______________________ Orlando has ________ comic books.

NAME ________________________

Lesson 2.6 Writing and Solving Two-Step Equations

Some problems with variables require more than one step to solve. Use the properties of equality to undo each step and find the value of the variable.

$2n - 7 = 19$

First, undo the subtraction by adding:

$2n - 7 + 7 = 19 + 7$ $\quad$ $2n = 26$

Then, undo the multiplication by dividing:

$\frac{2n}{2} = \frac{26}{2}$ $\quad$ $n = 13$

$\frac{n}{3} + 5 = 11$

First, undo the addition by subtracting:

$\frac{n}{3} + 5 - 5 = 11 - 5$ $\quad$ $\frac{n}{3} = 6$

Then, undo the division by multiplying:

$\frac{n}{3} \times 3 = 6 \times 3$ $\quad$ $n = 18$

Many word problems require two steps to solve.

Example: Maria bought three books and spent $48.15, including sales tax of $3.15. Each book cost the same amount. How much did each book cost?

$3x + 3.15 = 48.15$ $\quad$ $3x = 45$ $\quad$ $x = 15$

Find the value of the variable in each equation.

	a	b	c
1.	$3b + 4 = 13$ ________	$\frac{n}{4} - 2 = 2$ ________	$12p - 10 = 26$ ________
2.	$\frac{s}{4} + 6 = 9$ ________	$13 + \frac{a}{9} = 14$ ________	$7r + 3 = 31$ ________
3.	$\frac{x}{5} - 1 = 0$ ________	$5 = 2d - 5 =$ ________	$23 = 2t + 1$ ________

Write an equation for each problem. Then, solve the equation.

4. Kendra lost $\frac{1}{2}$ of her allowance, but her mother gave her 4 more dollars. Now she has $9. How much was her allowance?

____________________ Her allowance was $________.

5. Maria, Drew, and Justin all took part in a walk-a-thon. Together, they walked 9 miles. Justin walked 3 miles. Maria walked twice as far as Drew. How many miles did Drew walk?

____________________ Drew walked ________miles.

NAME ____________________

Check What You Learned

Integers and Equations

Add or subtract.

	a	b	c	d
1.	$13 + 11 =$ ______	$-13 + (-11) =$ ______	$13 + (-11) =$ ______	$-13 + 11 =$ ______
2.	$5 - 9 =$ ______	$-5 - 9 =$ ______	$5 - (-9) =$ ______	$-5 - (-9) =$ ______

Multiply or divide.

3.	$3 \times 8 =$ ______	$-3 \times 8 =$ ______	$3 \times (-8) =$ ______	$-3 \times (-8) =$ ______
4.	$9 \div 3 =$ ______	$9 \div (-3) =$ ______	$-9 \div 3 =$ ______	$-9 \div -3 =$ ______
5.	$6 \div (-1) =$ ______	$-6 \times (-1) =$ ______	$6 \div (-6) =$ ______	$-6 \div (-6) =$ ______

Rewrite each expression using the Distributive Property.

	a	b
6.	$7 \times (2 + 3) =$ ________	$(5 \times 6) + (5 \times 8) =$ ________
7.	$3 \times (6 - 2) =$ ________	$(9 \times 3) - (9 \times 4) =$ ________

Simplify each algebraic expression.

8. $2(4a + 3) + 3(5a + 4)$ ________

9. $6(b + 8) - 9(3b - 4)$ ________

10. $7(3c - 2) + 4(4 - c)$ ________

NAME ______________________________

Check What You Learned

Integers and Equations

CHAPTER 2 POSTTEST

Solve each equation.

	a	b	c
11.	$5 + t = 13$ ________	$s + 8 = 26$ ________	$31 = b + 27$ ________
12.	$42 - x = 29$ ________	$n - 9 = 22$ ________	$4 = 63 - z$ ________
13.	$r - 11 = 0$ ________	$c + 7 = 0$ ________	$2 = a - 9$ ________
14.	$5 \times t = 40$ ________	$s \times 8 = 48$ ________	$3b = 36$ ________
15.	$x \div 6 = 5$ ________	$81 \div n = 9$ ________	$\frac{z}{13} = 4$ ________
16.	$\frac{15}{r} = 3$ ________	$7 = \frac{c}{4}$ ________	$0 = 11a$ ________
17.	$4t + 2 = 22$ ________	$6s - 3 = 21$ ________	$\frac{b}{12} - 0 = 1$ ________

Write an equation for each problem. Then, solve the equation.

18. Jonas has 10 pencils. Three are red, and 2 are green. The rest are blue. How many blue pencils does he have?

______________________________ He has ________ blue pencils.

19. Nora spent $33 for 3 new T-shirts. If each T-shirt is the same price, how much did each T-shirt cost?

______________________________ Each T-shirt costs $________.

20. Trent had $20 to spend on 5 notebooks. After buying them, he had $7.50 left. How much did each notebook cost?

______________________________ Each notebook cost $________.

NAME ____________________

Check What You Know

Factors and Fractions

Find the greatest common factor of the two numbers.

	a	b	c
1.	12 and 39 ______	18 and 81 ______	14 and 70 ______

Find the prime factorization of each number below.

2.	52	98	108
	______	______	______

Rewrite each of the following using a base and exponent.

3.	$11 \times 11 =$ ______	$6 \times 6 \times 6 =$ ______	$c \times c \times c \times c =$ ______
4.	$r \times r \times r \times r \times r =$ ______	$39 \times 1 =$ ______	$(4)(4)(4)(4)(4)(4) =$ ______

Rewrite each of the following without a base and exponent.

5.	$10^6 =$ ______	$12^2 =$ ______	$43^1 =$ ______
6.	$5^3 =$ ______	$11^0 =$ ______	$3^4 =$ ______

Write each number in scientific notation.

7.	0.0042 = ______	420 = ______	42,000 = ______

Write each number in standard form.

8.	$7.25 \times 10^5 =$ ______	$7.25 \times 10^2 =$ ______	$7.25 \times 10^{-2} =$ ______

NAME ____________________

Check What You Know

Factors and Fractions

Solve the following equations.

	a	b	c
9.	$5^2 + 4^3 =$ ________	$(7 + 3)^2 =$ ________	$4^3 - 2^5 =$ ________
10.	$(9 - 4)^4 =$ ________	$3^3 - 3 =$ ________	$x + 9^2 = 90$ ________

Change each fraction to its simplest form. If the fraction is already in its simplest form, write *OK*.

	a	b
11.	$\frac{16}{24} =$ ________	$\frac{18}{48} =$ ________
12.	$\frac{20}{32} =$ ________	$\frac{13}{22} =$ ________

Simplify each algebraic fraction. If the fraction is already in its simplest form, write *OK*.

13.	$\frac{b^3}{ab^2} =$ ________	$\frac{6x}{12x^2} =$ ________
14.	$\frac{9s}{14r} =$ ________	$\frac{100c^2}{10c} =$ ________

Rewrite each multiplication or division expression using a base and an exponent.

15.	$7^4 \times 7^3 =$ ________	$(9 \times 9 \times 9 \times 9) \div (9 \times 9) =$ ________
16.	$5^{-10} \times 5^{-3} =$ ________	$6^5 \div 6^{-2} =$ ________

Use exponents to answer the question below.

17. If Serena puts $1,000 in a savings account that pays 2% interest compounded annually, how much money will she have in the account after 10 years? (Hint: To find the amount of money after 1 year, multiply by 1.02.)

She will have $ ________ in the account after 10 years.

NAME ______________________

Lesson 3.1 Prime Factorization and Greatest Common Factor

A **factor** is a divisor of a number. (For example, 3 and 4 are both factors of 12.) A common factor is a divisor shared by two or more numbers. The greatest common factor is the largest common factor shared by the numbers. To find the greatest common factor of two numbers, list all of the factors of each. For example, the factors of 32 are 1, 2, 4, 8, 16, and 32. The factors of 40 are 1, 2, 4, 5, 8, 10, 20, and 40. The greatest common factor is 8.

A **prime number** is any number greater than 1 that has only two factors, itself and 1. (Examples: 2, 3, 5, 7) A **composite number** has more than two factors. For example, 4 has three factors: 1, 2, and 4. A composite number can be written as a product of prime numbers. This is called the prime factorization of the number. For example, the **prime factorization** of 45 is 3, 3, 5. A factor tree like the one to the right can help determine the prime factorization of a number.

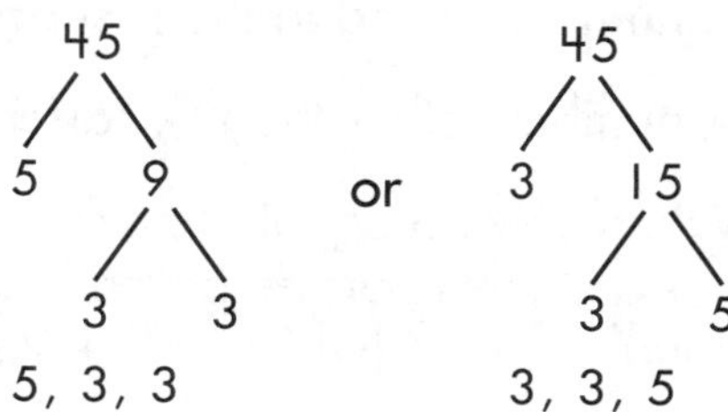

List the factors of each number below. Then, list the common factors and the greatest common factor.

	Factors	Common Factors	Greatest Common Factor
1.	9 ______	______	______
	15 ______		
2.	30 ______	______	______
	48 ______		

Use a factor tree to find the prime factorization of each number below.

	a	b
3.	54 ______	80 ______
4.	72 ______	60 ______

NAME ____________________

Lesson 3.2 Powers and Exponents

A number multiplied by itself can be written as follows: $2 \times 2 \times 2 \times 2 = 2^4 = 16$. In the expression 2^4, the small superscript 4 is called the **exponent**, and the 2 is called the **base**. An exponent is a number that indicates repeated multiplication. It shows how many times to multiply the base, the number that is being multiplied by itself. A number that can be expressed with a base and an exponent is called a **power**. For example, 2^4 is read as "2 to the 4th power." 2^2 is read as "2 to the 2nd power" or "2 squared." 2^3 is read as "2 to the 3rd power" or "2 cubed."

A number raised to the first power (n^1) is simply itself. For example, $2^1 = 2$.

A number, other than 0, raised to the 0 power (n^0) is 1. For example, $2^0 = 1$.

When solving equations with exponents, keep in mind that the Distributive Property does not apply to exponents outside parentheses. For example, $(2 + 5)^2 = (2 + 5)(2 + 5) = 7 \times 7 = 49$. It does not equal $2^2 + 5^2$ (which is $4 + 25$, or 29).

Rewrite each of the following using a base and exponent.

	a	b	c
1.	$5 \times 5 \times 5 =$ ________	$(3)(3)(3)(3)(3)(3) =$ ________	$b \times b \times b \times b =$ ________
2.	$23 \times 1 =$ ________	$n \times n \times n \times n \times n =$ ________	$12 \times 12 =$ ________

Rewrite each of the following without a base and exponent.

3.	$3^3 =$ ________	$11^2 =$ ________	$13^0 =$ ________
4.	$5^4 =$ ________	$10^5 =$ ________	$55^1 =$ ________

Solve the following equations.

	a	b	c	d
5.	$3^2 + 2^3 =$ ________	$(4 + 2)^2 =$ ________	$(5 - 1)^3 =$ ________	$3^3 - 5^2 =$ ________
6.	$3^4 + 6 =$ ________	$(3 + 1)^3 =$ ________	$2^5 - 10 =$ ________	$n + 7^2 = 50$ ________

NAME ____________________

Lesson 3.3 Simplifying Algebraic Fractions

A fraction is simplified, or reduced to lowest terms, when its numerator and denominator have no common factors other than 1. To simplify a fraction, divide the numerator and denominator by their greatest common factor.

Example: $\frac{60}{80} = \frac{(60 \div 20)}{(80 \div 20)} = \frac{3}{4}$

Algebraic fractions can also be simplified. Algebraic fractions are fractions with variables in the numerator and/or denominator.

Example: $\frac{12a^2}{15a} = \frac{(12a^2 \div 3a)}{(15a \div 3a)} = \frac{4a}{5}$

Write each fraction in simplest form. If the fraction is already in simplest form, write *OK*.

	a	b
1.	$\frac{18}{42}$ = ________	$\frac{48}{72}$ = ________
2.	$\frac{28}{32}$ = ________	$\frac{21}{35}$ = ________
3.	$\frac{15}{31}$ = ________	$\frac{27}{45}$ = ________
4.	$\frac{3}{27}$ = ________	$\frac{18}{30}$ = ________
5.	$\frac{26}{39}$ = ________	$\frac{12}{49}$ = ________

Simplify each algebraic fraction. If the fraction is already in simplest form, write *OK*.

6.	$\frac{9x}{18x^2}$ = ________	$\frac{14xy}{21xy^2}$ = ________
7.	$\frac{c^2}{c^3}$ = ________	$\frac{12ab}{15a^2b^2}$ = ________
8.	$\frac{25n^2}{55n}$ = ________	$\frac{7abc}{13a^2b^2}$ = ________
9.	$\frac{13x}{17y}$ = ________	$\frac{8sr}{20s}$ = ________
10.	$\frac{10b^2}{100b}$ = ________	$\frac{18p^2q^2}{81pq}$ = ________

NAME ____________________

Lesson 3.4 Multiplying and Dividing Powers

Use exponents to show how numbers with the same base are multiplied and divided:

$5^3 \times 5^3$ can be expressed as $5^{3+3} = 5^6$ because it means $(5 \times 5 \times 5) \times (5 \times 5 \times 5)$.

$10^6 \div 10^2$ can be expressed as $10^{6-2} = 10^4$ because it means $(10 \times 10 \times 10 \times 10 \times 10 \times 10) \div (10 \times 10)$

Rewrite each multiplication or division expression using a base and an exponent.

	a	b
1.	$(4 \times 4 \times 4) \times (4 \times 4) =$ ________	$7^2 \times 7^3 =$ ________
2.	$(8 \times 8 \times 8 \times 8) \div (8 \times 8) =$ ________	$4^9 \div 4^5 =$ ________
3.	$3^3 \times 3^5 =$ ________	$(6 \times 6) \times (6 \times 6) =$ ________
4.	$9^6 \div 9^3 =$ ________	$8 \times 8^5 =$ ________
5.	$(5 \times 5 \times 5 \times 5) \div (5 \times 5) =$ ________	$12^3 \times 12 =$ ________
6.	$5^5 \div 5 =$ ________	$10^5 \times 10^2 =$ ________
7.	$2^3 \times 2^5 =$ ________	$3^{11} \div 3^6 =$ ________
8.	$11^5 \div 11^2 =$ ________	$(2 \times 2 \times 2) \div 2 =$ ________

Use exponents to answer the questions below.

9. If a town with a population of 3,000 grows by 2% per year, how large will the population be in 10 years? (Hint: To find the population after 1 year, multiply by 1.02).

   The town's population will be ________ after 10 years.

10. How many times more people will there be in the town after 15 years than after 10 years?

    There will be ________ times more people after 15 years.

NAME ______________________

Lesson 3.5 Negative Exponents

A **negative exponent** can be written with the base of the denominator in a fraction where the numerator is 1. The exponent then becomes positive.

5^{-3} means $\frac{1}{5^3} = \frac{1}{125} = 0.008$ $\quad$ 10^{-2} means $\frac{1}{10^2} = \frac{1}{100} = 0.01$

It is possible to multiply and divide numbers with positive and negative exponents that have the same base.

$5^{-3} \times 5^{-2} = 5^{-3+(-2)} = 5^{-5}$ $\quad$ $4^{-3} \div 4^{-2} = 4^{-3-(-2)} = 4^{-3+2} = 4^{-1}$

$6^{-4} \times 6^{2} = 6^{-4+2} = 6^{-2}$ $\quad$ $8^{4} \div 8^{-3} = 8^{4-(-3)} = 8^{4+3} = 8^{7}$

Rewrite each multiplication or division expression using a base and an exponent.

	a	b
1.	$10^{-12} \times 10^{-4} =$ ________	$9^{5} \div 9^{-3} =$ ________
2.	$2^{-3} \times 2^{2} =$ ________	$6^{-5} \times 6^{-4} =$ ________
3.	$3^{-4} \div 3 =$ ________	$2^{-5} \div 2^{3} =$ ________
4.	$5^{-5} \times 5^{-4} =$ ________	$7^{4} \times 7^{-3} =$ ________
5.	$12^{-3} \div 12^{3} =$ ________	$8^{6} \div 8^{-3} =$ ________
6.	$6^{-6} \times 6^{4} =$ ________	$11^{-3} \times 11^{-4} =$ ________
7.	$2^{5} \times 2^{-6} =$ ________	$7^{3} \div 7^{-2} =$ ________
8.	$4^{-3} \div 4^{-5} =$ ________	$12^{-4} \times 12^{-6} =$ ________

Use negative exponents to answer the questions below.

9. A dust mite is about 250 microns long. One micron equals 0.001 millimeter. How long is a dust mite in millimeters?

   A dust mite is ________ millimeters long.

10. If a pinhead is about 2.5 millimeters in diameter, how much larger is the pinhead than a dust mite?

    The pinhead is about ________ times larger than a dust mite.

NAME ____________________

Lesson 3.6 Scientific Notation

Scientific notation is most often used as a concise way of writing very large and small numbers. It involves writing a number between 1 and 10 multiplied by a power of 10. Any number can be written in scientific notation.

$1{,}503 = 1.503 \times 10^3$ (+3)

$0.0376 = 3.76 \times 10^{-2}$ (−2)

$85 = 8.5 \times 10$ (+1)

Translate numbers written in scientific notation into standard form by reading the exponent.

$7.03 \times 10^5 = 703000$ Add 5 places.

$5.4 \times 10^{-4} = 0.00054$ Subtract 4 places.

Write each number in scientific notation.

	a	b	c
1.	38.4 ________	6,210 ________	0.031 ________
2.	47,165 ________	0.00076 ________	367.32 ________
3.	0.795 ________	921.5 ________	61,321 ________

Write each number in standard form.

4.	4.17×10^{-5} = ______	2.07×10^{3} = ______	9.36×10^{-4} = ______
5.	9.55×10^{2} = ______	6.26×10^{-2} = ______	8.13×10^{4} = ______
6.	5.76×10^{-1} = ______	7.57×10^{5} = ______	3.7×10^{-3} = ______

Use scientific notation to answer the questions below.

7. Earth is about 384,400 kilometers from the moon. What is this distance in scientific notation?

Earth is about ________________ kilometers from the moon.

8. Earth is about 150 million kilometers from the sun. What is this distance in scientific notation?

Earth is about ________________ kilometers from the sun.

NAME ________________________

Check What You Learned

Factors and Fractions

Find the greatest common factor of the two numbers.

	a	b	c
1.	14 and 21 ________	15 and 36 ________	28 and 40 ________

Find the prime factorization of each number below.

2.	48	42	120
	________	________	________

Rewrite each of the following using a base and exponent.

3.	$15 \times 15 =$ ________	$(5)(5)(5)(5)(5)(5) =$ ________	$9 \times 9 \times 9 \times 9 =$ ________
4.	$17 \times 1 =$ ________	$s \times s \times s =$ ________	$q \times q \times q \times q \times q =$ ________

Rewrite each of the following without a base and exponent.

5.	$2^6 =$ ________	$13^2 =$ ________	$23^1 =$ ________
6.	$4^3 =$ ________	$93^0 =$ ________	$10^4 =$ ________

Write each number in scientific notation.

7.	$0.0027 =$ ________	$27 =$ ________	$2{,}700 =$ ________

Write each number in standard form.

8.	$6.14 \times 10^4 =$ ________	$6.14 \times 10^{-2} =$ ________	$6.14 \times 10^{-4} =$ ________

NAME ___

Check What You Learned

Factors and Fractions

Solve the following equations.

	a	b	c
9.	$5^3 + 2^4 =$ ___	$(8 + 4)^2 =$ ___	$7^2 - 3^3 =$ ___
10.	$(6 - 4)^5 =$ ___	$10^3 - 10 =$ ___	$b + 4^3 = 70$ ___

Change each fraction to its simplest form. If the fraction is already in its simplest form, write *OK*.

	a	b
11.	$\frac{20}{36} =$ ___	$\frac{17}{34} =$ ___
12.	$\frac{9}{20} =$ ___	$\frac{24}{42} =$ ___

Simplify each algebraic fraction. If the fraction is already in its simplest form, write *OK*.

13.	$\frac{7p}{24q} =$ ___	$\frac{12mn}{18mn^2} =$ ___
14.	$\frac{12b}{144b^2} =$ ___	$\frac{5a^2b^2c}{15ab} =$ ___

Rewrite each multiplication or division expression using a base and an exponent.

15.	$8^{11} \times 8^4 =$ ___	$(3 \times 3 \times 3 \times 3 \times 3) \div (3 \times 3 \times 3) =$ ___
16.	$3^{-6} \times 3^4 =$ ___	$11^6 \div 11^{-6} =$ ___

Use exponents to answer the questions below.

17. If Lucas puts $1,500 in a savings account that pays 3% interest compounded annually, how much money will he have in the account after 5 years? (Hint: To find the amount of money after 1 year, multiply by 1.03.)

He will have $ ___ in the account after 5 years.

NAME ____________________

Check What You Know

Rational Numbers

Change each of the following to a decimal as indicated.

	a	b	c
1.	Change $\frac{4}{5}$ to tenths. ________	Change $\frac{7}{20}$ to hundredths. ________	Change $\frac{14}{125}$ to thousandths. ________
2.	Change $2\frac{3}{4}$ to hundredths. ________	Change $1\frac{7}{25}$ to hundredths. ________	Change $1\frac{7}{8}$ to thousandths. ________

Change the improper fractions to mixed numerals and the mixed numerals to improper fractions.

	a	b	c	d
3.	$\frac{27}{2}$ = ________	$\frac{14}{9}$ = ________	$\frac{32}{5}$ = ________	$\frac{83}{10}$ = ________
4.	$\frac{28}{13}$ = ________	$\frac{40}{3}$ = ________	$1\frac{7}{8}$ = ________	$2\frac{9}{10}$ = ________
5.	$3\frac{3}{4}$ = ________	$4\frac{1}{5}$ = ________	$5\frac{2}{3}$ = ________	$6\frac{2}{5}$ = ________

Add or subtract. Write each sum or difference in simplest form.

	a	b	c	d
6.	$\frac{2}{3} + \frac{3}{8}$	$\frac{10}{11} + \frac{1}{4}$	$3\frac{5}{8} + \frac{2}{5}$	$4\frac{5}{6} + 2\frac{2}{7}$
7.	$\frac{11}{12} - \frac{3}{4}$	$\frac{7}{8} - \frac{1}{2}$	$5\frac{6}{7} - \frac{3}{10}$	$3\frac{1}{3} - 2\frac{1}{4}$

NAME ______________________

Check What You Know

Rational Numbers

Multiply or divide. Write each product or quotient in simplest form.

	a	b	c
8.	$\frac{3}{10} \times \frac{4}{5} =$ ________	$2\frac{7}{8} \times \frac{1}{3} =$ ________	$5\frac{1}{6} \times 2\frac{3}{7} =$ ________
9.	$\frac{2}{5} \div \frac{1}{4} =$ ________	$3 \div \frac{2}{9} =$ ________	$3\frac{1}{3} \div 2\frac{1}{4} =$ ________

Solve the following equations. Write each answer in simplest form.

10. $m + 3.4 = 7.9$ ________ $n - 6.3 = 9$ ________ $p - (-\frac{6}{7}) = \frac{13}{14}$ ________

11. $8t = \frac{1}{9}$ ________ $s \times \frac{3}{4} = -20$ ________ $-10.5r = -31.5$ ________

Find the next number in each of the following sequences.

12. 3, 5.5, 8, 10.5, 13, ________

13. 4, 12, 36, 108, 324, ________

Solve the following equations.

14. Ella has gold, silver, and copper wire for stringing beads. She has $1\frac{1}{2}$ ft. of gold wire, $2\frac{1}{3}$ ft. of silver wire, and $3\frac{3}{4}$ ft. of copper wire. How much wire does she have altogether?

She has ________ ft. of wire.

15. Green Valley Middle School wants to raise $7,500 for new equipment. If grades 6 and 7 each raise $2,450.25, how much money does grade 8 need to raise?

Grade 8 needs to raise $________.

NAME ______________________

Lesson 4.1 Changing Fractions to Decimals

Change $\frac{1}{5}$ to tenths.

$\frac{1}{5} = \frac{1 \times 2}{5 \times 2} = \frac{2}{10} = 0.2$

Change $\frac{1}{4}$ to hundredths.

$\frac{1}{4} = \frac{1 \times 25}{4 \times 25} = \frac{25}{100} = 0.25$

Change $\frac{1}{5}$ to hundredths.

$\frac{1}{5} = \frac{1 \times 20}{5 \times 20} = \frac{20}{100} = 0.20$

Change $3\frac{1}{250}$ to thousandths.

$3\frac{1}{250} = 3\frac{1 \times 4}{250 \times 4} = 3\frac{4}{1000} = 3.004$

Change each of the following to a decimal as indicated.

	a	b	c
1.	Change $\frac{3}{5}$ to tenths. ______	Change $\frac{3}{5}$ to hundredths. ______	Change $\frac{3}{5}$ to thousandths. ______
2.	Change $5\frac{1}{5}$ to tenths. ______	Change $\frac{3}{20}$ to hundredths. ______	Change $\frac{12}{125}$ to thousandths. ______
3.	Change $4\frac{4}{5}$ to tenths. ______	Change $3\frac{11}{20}$ to hundredths. ______	Change $2\frac{7}{40}$ to thousandths. ______

Solve each problem. Write each answer as a fraction and then as a decimal.

4. To make one recipe, Lina needs $\frac{1}{4}$ cup of sugar. For another recipe, she needs $\frac{1}{2}$ cup of sugar. How much sugar does she need for both recipes?

Lina needs ________ cup of sugar. Written as a decimal, this is ________ cup of sugar.

5. A table is $6\frac{1}{2}$ ft. long. Its tablecloth is $7\frac{3}{4}$ ft. long. How much longer is the tablecloth than the table?

The tablecloth is ________ ft. longer than the table. Written as a decimal, this is ________ ft.

NAME ______________________

Lesson 4.2 Rational Numbers

A number that can be written as the ratio of two integers is called a **rational number**. For example, the fraction $\frac{1}{3}$ is a rational number because it is the ratio 1 to 3. The number 2 is a rational number because it can be written as $\frac{2}{1}$, or the ratio of 2 to 1. A decimal is also a rational number because it can be written as a fraction. For example, $0.234 = \frac{234}{1{,}000}$.

A fraction whose numerator is greater than its denominator is called an **improper fraction**. An improper fraction can be changed to a **mixed numeral**, a number written as a whole number and a fraction. To change an improper fraction to a mixed numeral, divide the numerator by the denominator. For example, $\frac{18}{7}$ means $18 \div 7$. Because 7 divides into 18 two times with a remainder of 4, $\frac{18}{7}$ equals $2\frac{4}{7}$.

To change a mixed numeral into an improper fraction, multiply the whole number by the denominator and add the numerator. Place this number over the denominator.
For example, $4\frac{3}{5} = \frac{(4 \times 5) + 3}{5} = \frac{23}{5}$

Change the improper fractions to mixed numerals.

	a	b	c	d
1.	$\frac{23}{2}$ = ______	$\frac{17}{9}$ = ______	$\frac{29}{5}$ = ______	$\frac{71}{3}$ = ______
2.	$\frac{45}{4}$ = ______	$\frac{142}{15}$ = ______	$\frac{100}{33}$ = ______	$\frac{55}{7}$ = ______

Change the mixed numerals to improper fractions.

3.	$4\frac{1}{3}$ = ______	$5\frac{4}{9}$ = ______	$2\frac{4}{5}$ = ______	$3\frac{2}{7}$ = ______
4.	$7\frac{1}{4}$ = ______	$9\frac{5}{6}$ = ______	$6\frac{2}{9}$ = ______	$8\frac{3}{8}$ = ______

NAME ____________________

Lesson 4.3 Multiplying and Dividing Fractions and Mixed Numerals

To multiply fractions, multiply numerators and then denominators. Then, simplify.

Examples:

$$\frac{3}{5} \times \frac{1}{6} = \frac{3 \times 1}{5 \times 6} = \frac{3}{30} = \frac{1}{10}$$

$$2\frac{1}{5} \times \frac{3}{4} \times \frac{1}{6} = \frac{11}{5} \times \frac{3}{4} \times \frac{1}{6} = \frac{11 \times 3 \times 1}{5 \times 4 \times 6} = \frac{33}{120} = \frac{11}{40}$$

To divide a fraction, multiply by its **reciprocal**. The product of a number and its reciprocal is 1. To make a reciprocal, reverse the numerator and denominator. For example, $\frac{3}{5}$ and $\frac{5}{3}$ are reciprocals, because $\frac{3}{5} \times \frac{5}{3} = \frac{15}{15} = 1$.

Examples:

$$\frac{3}{5} \div \frac{1}{4} = \frac{3}{5} \times \frac{4}{1} = \frac{12}{5} = 2\frac{2}{5}$$

reciprocals

$$12 \div 2\frac{1}{4} = \frac{12}{1} \div \frac{9}{4} = \frac{12}{1} \times \frac{4}{9} = \frac{48}{9} = 5\frac{1}{3}$$

reciprocals

Multiply or divide. Write each product or quotient in simplest form.

	a	b	c
1.	$\frac{3}{7} \times \frac{2}{3}$ = ________	$\frac{5}{6} \times \frac{3}{4}$ = ________	$\frac{4}{5} \times \frac{1}{2}$ = ________
2.	$2\frac{1}{3} \times \frac{2}{5}$ = ________	$3\frac{4}{9} \times 1\frac{1}{4}$ = ________	$5\frac{2}{7} \times 2\frac{1}{6}$ = ________
3.	$\frac{1}{9} \times \frac{2}{7} \times \frac{3}{8}$ = ________	$3 \times \frac{2}{9} \times \frac{1}{5}$ = ________	$1\frac{7}{8} \times 1\frac{3}{7} \times \frac{1}{2}$ = ________
4.	$\frac{5}{7} \div \frac{1}{4}$ = ________	$\frac{3}{4} \div \frac{2}{5}$ = ________	$\frac{1}{8} \div \frac{2}{3}$ = ________
5.	$4 \div \frac{2}{5}$ = ________	$5 \div 1\frac{1}{2}$ = ________	$7 \div 2\frac{1}{3}$ = ________
6.	$2\frac{1}{8} \div 4$ = ________	$3\frac{2}{3} \div 1\frac{2}{5}$ = ________	$4\frac{3}{5} \div 2\frac{1}{6}$ = ________

NAME ____________________

Lesson 4.4 Adding and Subtracting Fractions and Mixed Numerals

To add or subtract fractions or mixed numerals with different denominators, give all of the fractions the same denominator. Give fractions the same denominators by finding the least common multiple of their denominators. The **least common multiple** of two numbers is the smallest number that is a multiple of both. For example, the multiples of 4 are 4, 8, 12, 16, 20, and so on. The multiples of 5 are 5, 10, 15, 20, and so on. The least common multiple of 4 and 5 is 20.

Example:

$$7\tfrac{1}{6} \rightarrow 7\tfrac{5}{30} \rightarrow 6 + 1 + \tfrac{5}{30} \rightarrow 6 + \tfrac{30}{30} + \tfrac{5}{30} = 6\tfrac{35}{30}$$

$$-1\tfrac{2}{5} \rightarrow 1\tfrac{12}{30} \longrightarrow -1\tfrac{12}{30}$$

$$5\tfrac{23}{30}$$

Add or subtract. Write each sum or difference in simplest form.

	a	b	c	d
1.	$\frac{3}{4} + \frac{2}{5}$	$\frac{7}{8} + \frac{4}{9}$	$\frac{5}{6} + \frac{2}{3}$	$\frac{14}{15} + \frac{3}{10}$
2.	$\frac{8}{9} - \frac{1}{3}$	$\frac{4}{5} - \frac{1}{2}$	$\frac{9}{10} - \frac{3}{4}$	$\frac{15}{16} - \frac{7}{10}$
3.	$3\frac{1}{4} + 1\frac{2}{3}$	$2\frac{2}{5} + \frac{1}{4}$	$6\frac{7}{8} - 3\frac{1}{4}$	$4\frac{1}{6} - 2\frac{1}{5}$
4.	$\frac{2}{3} + \frac{3}{4} + \frac{4}{5}$	$\frac{2}{5} + \frac{5}{8} + 1\frac{1}{3}$	$2\frac{1}{4} + 5\frac{3}{5} + \frac{1}{6}$	$1\frac{1}{2} + 2\frac{1}{3} + 3\frac{1}{4}$

NAME ____________________

Lesson 4.5 Solving Equations with Rational Numbers

To solve an equation with rational numbers, you must find a value that makes the variable in the equation true. To do this, use inverse operations to rearrange the equation so that the variable is alone on one side. **Inverse operations** are operations that have the opposite effect, like addition and subtraction or multiplication and division. Remember that whatever you do to one side of the equation, you must also do to the other side of the equation.

Examples:

$a + 2.4 = 6.5$

$a + 2.4 - 2.4 = 6.5 - 2.4$

$a = 4.1$

$\frac{3x}{4} = \frac{2}{3}$

$\frac{4}{3}\left(\frac{3x}{4}\right) = \frac{2}{3}\left(\frac{4}{3}\right)$

$x = \frac{8}{9}$

Solve the following equations. Write each equation in simplest form.

	a	b	c
1.	$x + 4.1 = 6.5$ ________	$y - 7.8 = 12$ ________	$-5.4 + z = 10.2$ ________
2.	$a + \frac{2}{5} = \frac{9}{10}$ ________	$b - 1\frac{3}{4} = 4\frac{1}{4}$ ________	$c - (-\frac{2}{3}) = \frac{5}{6}$ ________
3.	$2.3m = -4.6$ ________	$-4n = 3.8$ ________	$-7.6p = -22.8$ ________
4.	$15r = \frac{1}{3}$ ________	$s \times \frac{7}{8} = -10$ ________	$\frac{t}{12} = \frac{1}{6}$ ________

Write an equation for each problem. Then, solve the equation.

5. Loreena needs $4\frac{1}{2}$ ft. of yellow yarn for a craft project. She already has $3\frac{3}{8}$ ft. How much more yarn does she need to buy?

She needs to buy ________ ft. of yarn.

6. Jaime makes $8.20 an hour in his part-time job. He made $53.30 last week. How many hours did he work?

He worked ________ hours.

NAME ____________________

Lesson 4.6 Arithmetic and Geometric Sequences

An **arithmetic sequence** is a list of numbers that follows a pattern of adding or subtracting the same amount from one number to the next. For example, 2, 6, 10, 14, 18, ... is an arithmetic sequence because you add 4 at each step. A **geometric sequence** is a list of numbers that follows a pattern of multiplying or dividing by the same amount from one number to the next. For example, 1, 3, 9, 27, 81, ... is a geometric sequence because you multiply by 3 at each step.

In an arithmetic sequence, the number that is added or subtracted at each step is called the **common difference**. For example, in the sequence 2, 6, 10, 14, 18, ... , the common difference is 4. In a geometric sequence, the number that is multiplied or divided at each step is called the **common ratio**. For example, in the sequence 1, 3, 9, 27, 81, ... , the common ratio is 3.

Find the common difference and the next number in each of the following sequences.

		Common Difference	Next Number
1.	1, 6, 11, 16, 21, ...	______	______
2.	99, 88, 77, 66, 55, ...	______	______
3.	10, 9.5, 9, 8.5, 8, ...	______	______
4.	4, $3\frac{1}{3}$, $2\frac{2}{3}$, 2, $1\frac{1}{3}$, ...	______	______
5.	3, 10.5, 18, 25.5, 33, ...	______	______

Find the common ratio and the next number in each of the following sequences.

		Common Ratio	Next Number
6.	2, 12, 72, 432, 2,592, ...	______	______
7.	1,000, 500, 250, 125, 62.5, ...	______	______
8.	$\frac{1}{10}$, 1, 10, 100, 1,000, ...	______	______
9.	2.5, 7.5, 22.5, 67.5, 202.5, ...	______	______
10.	2,401, 343, 49, 7, 1, ...	______	______

NAME ______________________

Check What You Learned

Rational Numbers

Change each of the following to a decimal as indicated.

	a	b	c
1.	Change $\frac{2}{5}$ to tenths. ________	Change $\frac{13}{25}$ to hundredths. ________	Change $\frac{43}{250}$ to thousandths. ________
2.	Change $6\frac{9}{25}$ to hundredths. ________	Change $5\frac{49}{50}$ to hundredths. ________	Change $3\frac{1}{8}$ to thousandths. ________

Change the improper fractions to mixed numerals and the mixed numerals to improper fractions.

	a	b	c	d
3.	$\frac{25}{2}$ = ________	$\frac{13}{9}$ = ________	$\frac{51}{5}$ = ________	$\frac{22}{3}$ = ________
4.	$\frac{60}{11}$ = ________	$\frac{47}{10}$ = ________	$9\frac{1}{3}$ = ________	$8\frac{1}{2}$ = ________
5.	$7\frac{2}{5}$ = ________	$6\frac{5}{7}$ = ________	$5\frac{5}{8}$ = ________	$4\frac{5}{9}$ = ________

Add or subtract. Write each sum or difference in simplest form.

	a	b	c	d
6.	$\frac{5}{9} + \frac{4}{5}$	$\frac{6}{7} + \frac{1}{3}$	$4\frac{7}{8} + \frac{3}{4}$	$2\frac{9}{10} + 3\frac{2}{5}$
7.	$\frac{10}{11} - \frac{7}{8}$	$\frac{7}{10} - \frac{2}{3}$	$10\frac{1}{4} - \frac{3}{7}$	$9\frac{1}{9} - 8\frac{1}{8}$

NAME ______________________

Check What You Learned

Rational Numbers

CHAPTER 4 POSTTEST

Multiply or divide. Write each product or quotient in simplest form.

	a	b	c
8.	$\frac{7}{8} \times \frac{3}{4} =$ ________	$1\frac{2}{5} \times \frac{1}{6} =$ ________	$3\frac{3}{7} \times 2\frac{4}{5} =$ ________
9.	$\frac{3}{8} \div \frac{1}{5} =$ ________	$6 \div \frac{3}{5} =$ ________	$5\frac{1}{4} \div 3\frac{1}{8} =$ ________

Solve the following equations. Write each answer in simplest form.

10. $b + 5.2 = 9.5$ ________ $c - 7.7 = 10$ ________ $d - (-\frac{7}{8}) = \frac{15}{16}$ ________

11. $5x = \frac{1}{4}$ ________ $y \times \frac{5}{6} = -3$ ________ $-4.2z = -14.7$ ________

Find the next number in each of the following sequences.

12. 2, 5.5, 9, 12.5, 16, ________

13. 12, $11\frac{2}{3}$, $11\frac{1}{3}$, 11, $10\frac{2}{3}$, ________

Write an equation for each problem. Then, solve the equation.

14. Cristina has $1\frac{1}{4}$ loaves of white bread, $2\frac{1}{3}$ loaves of wheat bread, and $1\frac{1}{2}$ loaves of multigrain bread. How many loaves of bread does she have altogether?

She has ________ loaves of bread.

15. Ryan has $100 to buy new clothes. If he buys 3 shirts that cost $29.23 each, including taxes, how much money will he have left?

He will have $________ left.

NAME ______________________

Check What You Know

Proportion, Percent, and Interest

Circle the proportions that are true. Show your work.

	a	b	c
1.	$\frac{6}{8} = \frac{12}{16}$	$\frac{3}{7} = \frac{9}{24}$	$\frac{4}{5} = \frac{20}{25}$
2.	$\frac{5}{3} = \frac{16}{9}$	$\frac{3}{5} = \frac{21}{35}$	$\frac{9}{10} = \frac{15}{20}$

Solve the *n* in each proportion.

3. $\frac{4}{n} = \frac{28}{35}$ ________ $\frac{2}{3} = \frac{16}{n}$ ________ $\frac{n}{9} = \frac{45}{81}$ ________

4. $\frac{11}{12} = \frac{n}{36}$ ________ $\frac{10}{n} = \frac{18}{27}$ ________ $\frac{42}{24} = \frac{7}{n}$ ________

For each fraction or mixed numeral, write the equivalent percent. For each percent, write the equivalent fraction or mixed numeral.

5. 7% = ________ ________% = $\frac{9}{20}$ 170% = ________

6. ________% = $4\frac{2}{5}$ $4\frac{1}{2}$% = ________ ________% = $\frac{7}{25}$

For each decimal, write the equivalent percent. For each percent, write the equivalent decimal.

7. 3.12% = ________ ________% = 0.234 72% = ________

8. ________% = 0.075 195% = ________ ________% = 0.0055

NAME ______________________

Check What You Know

Proportion, Percent, and Interest

Complete each sentence.

	a	b
9.	28% of 150 is ________.	90 is ________% of 180.
10.	54 is 60% of ________.	________ is 15% more than 20.

Fill in the missing information about each loan.

	Principal	Rate	Time	Compounded	Interest	Total Amount
11.	\$4,000	________	2 years	no	\$320	\$4,320
12.	\$1,500	$6\frac{1}{2}$%	________	no	\$292.50	\$1,792.50
13.	\$600	7%	4 years	no	________	________
14.	________	5%	$2\frac{1}{2}$ years	no	\$437.50	________
15.	\$2,000	$4\frac{1}{4}$%	3 years	annually	________	________
16.	\$800	2%	2 years	semi-annually	________	________

Solve each problem.

17. Isabel biked 4 miles in 15 minutes. At that rate, how far will she bike in 45 minutes?

She will bike ________ miles.

18. All shirts on the clearance rack are 60% off. If one of the shirts was originally \$29.95, how much does it cost now?

The shirt costs \$________ now.

NAME ___________________________

Lesson 5.1 Ratio and Proportion

A **ratio** is a comparison of two numbers. A ratio can be expressed as 1 to 2, 1:2, or $\frac{1}{2}$, and it means that for every 1 of the first item, there are 2 of the other item. For example, 2 dollars per gallon is a ratio. For every 1 gallon you buy, you pay 2 dollars.

A **proportion** expresses the equality of two ratios. To check if a proportion is true, cross-multiply to determine if the two ratios are equal.

$\frac{4}{2} \times \frac{2}{1}$ $\frac{4}{2} = \frac{2}{1}$ $4 \times 1 = 2 \times 2$, so it is true. $\frac{3}{4} = \frac{2}{3}$ $3 \times 3 \neq 4 \times 2$, so it is **not** true.

Circle the proportions that are true. Show your work.

	a	b	c
1.	$\frac{1}{4} = \frac{2}{8}$	$\frac{1}{3} = \frac{4}{9}$	$\frac{2}{7} = \frac{6}{21}$
2.	$\frac{9}{4} = \frac{27}{16}$	$\frac{3}{25} = \frac{12}{100}$	$\frac{4}{5} = \frac{12}{20}$
3.	$\frac{1}{11} = \frac{3}{30}$	$\frac{8}{3} = \frac{24}{9}$	$\frac{15}{25} = \frac{3}{5}$
4.	$\frac{8}{9} = \frac{72}{81}$	$\frac{7}{8} = \frac{49}{64}$	$\frac{11}{12} = \frac{20}{24}$

The picture, table, and graph below all illustrate the same ratio.

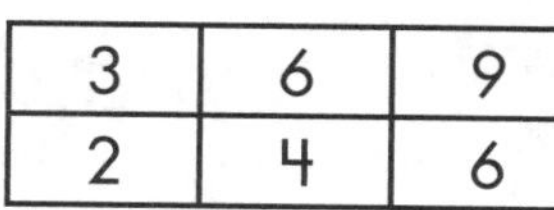

3	6	9
2	4	6

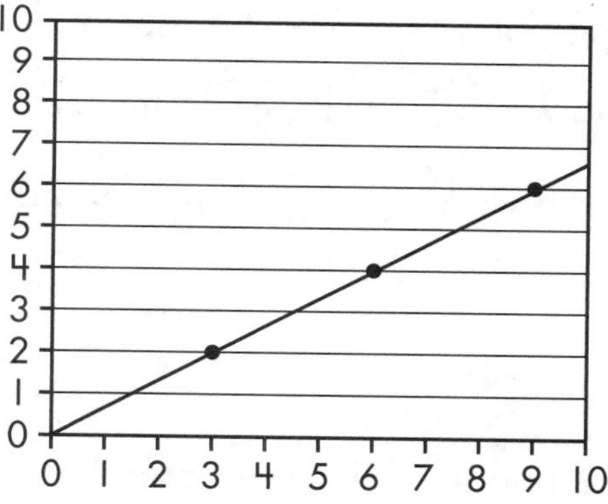

5. Which fraction expresses this ratio in simplest form? Circle the correct answer.

a. $\frac{3}{6}$ b. $\frac{3}{4}$ c. $\frac{3}{2}$

NAME ______________________________

Lesson 5.2 Solving Proportion Equations

To find the unknown number in a proportion, first cross-multiply to make an equation. Then, divide both sides by the number with *n*.

$\frac{4}{5} = \frac{n}{15}$ $4 \times 15 = 5 \times n$ $60 \div 5 = 5n \div 5$

$60 = 5n$ $12 = n$

In proportion problems, two things change at the same rate. Example: The Longs drove 680 miles in 2 days. At that rate, how far will they drive in 5 days?

Let *n* equal the unknown number—in this case, how far the Longs will drive in 5 days. Set up a proportion. For example, compare the number of days to the number of miles, or the number of miles to the number of days. Whichever you choose, do the same for both sides of the proportion. Then, cross-multiply to solve.

$\frac{2}{5} = \frac{680}{n}$ or $\frac{680}{2} = \frac{n}{5}$ In each case, $n = 1{,}700$

Solve for *n* in each proportion.

	a	b	c
1.	$\frac{2}{3} = \frac{n}{15}$ ____________	$\frac{n}{7} = \frac{16}{28}$ ____________	$\frac{14}{10} = \frac{21}{n}$ ____________
2.	$\frac{35}{15} = \frac{n}{3}$ ____________	$\frac{11}{n} = \frac{33}{30}$ ____________	$\frac{3}{4} = \frac{n}{100}$ ____________
3.	$\frac{n}{2} = \frac{33}{66}$ ____________	$\frac{9}{10} = \frac{81}{n}$ ____________	$\frac{20}{n} = \frac{1}{5}$ ____________
4.	$\frac{36}{6} = \frac{6}{n}$ ____________	$\frac{n}{9} = \frac{14}{18}$ ____________	$\frac{13}{n} = \frac{26}{22}$ ____________

Use a proportion to solve each problem.

5. Marta walked 2 miles in 28 minutes. At that rate, how far can she walk in 70 minutes?

She can walk ________ miles in 70 minutes.

6. On a map, each inch represents 20 miles. If two cities are 5 inches apart on the map, how far apart are the two cities in miles?

They are ________ miles apart.

NAME ____________________

Lesson 5.3 Understanding Percents

Percent (%) means "out of 100."

Examples: 1 percent (1%) = 0.01 = $\frac{1}{100}$. 125% = 1.25 = $1\frac{25}{100}$ = $1\frac{1}{4}$

Use this method to change a percent into a fraction:

$12\% = \frac{12}{100} \div \frac{4}{4} = \frac{3}{25}$

Use this method to change a decimal to a percent:

$0.165 = \frac{16.5}{100} = 16.5\%$

Use this method to change a fraction into a percent:

$\frac{5}{8} = \frac{n}{100}$ $\quad 500 = 8n \quad$ $62\frac{1}{2}\% = n$

Use this method to change a percent to a decimal:

$49.5\% = \frac{49.5}{100} = 0.495$

For each fraction or mixed numeral, write the equivalent percent. For each percent, write the equivalent fraction or mixed numeral.

	a	b	c
1.	20% = ______	______% = $\frac{3}{8}$	120% = ______
2.	______% = $2\frac{5}{8}$	82% = ______	$14\frac{1}{4}\%$ = ______
3.	164% = ______	______% = $\frac{7}{20}$	______% = $\frac{4}{25}$
4.	______% = $\frac{19}{20}$	248% = ______	______% = $3\frac{3}{10}$

For each decimal, write the equivalent percent. For each percent, write the equivalent decimal.

5.	5.75% = ______	______% = 0.125	58% = ______
6.	______% = 1.15	9% = ______	______% = 0.035
7.	225% = ______	______% = 0.005	99% = ______
8.	______% = 0.8	______% = 3.82	52.25% = ______

NAME ____________________

Lesson 5.4 Finding Percent

What number is $17\frac{1}{2}\%$ of 80?

$17\frac{1}{2}\%$ of 80 = 17.5% × 80

0.175 × 80 = 14

$17\frac{1}{2}\%$ of 80 is 14.

50 is what percent of 80?

$50 = n\% \times 80$ $50 = \frac{n}{100} \times 80$

$50 = 80\frac{n}{100}$ $5{,}000 = 80n$

$5{,}000 \div 80 = 80n \div 80$

$62.5 = n$ 50 is 62.5% of 80.

15 is 30% of what number?

$15 = 30\% \times n$

$15 = \frac{30}{100} \times n$

$15 = \frac{3n}{10}$ $150 = 3n$

$50 = n$ 15 is 30% of 50.

What number is 5% more than 950?

950 + 5% of 950 = 950 + (5% × 950) =

950 + (0.05 × 950) = 950 + 47.50 = 997.50

997.50 is 5% more than 950.

102 is what percent less than 120?

120 − 102 = 18 $18 = n\%$ *of* 120

$18 = n \times 120$ $\frac{18}{120} = n$

$0.15 = n$ 102 is 15% less than 120.

Complete each sentence.

	a	b
1.	15% of 125 is ________.	14 is ________% of 112.
2.	24 is 40% of ________.	________ is 3% more than 70.
3.	7.2 is ________% of 3.6.	110 is 25% of ________.
4.	________ is 15% less than 60.	77 is ________% more than 70.

Solve each problem.

5. All winter jackets are on sale for 75% off. If a jacket originally cost $90, how much does it cost now?

The jacket now costs $________.

6. Marcus went on a diet and now weighs 140 lbs. He originally weighed 175 lbs. What percent of his weight did he lose?

He lost ________% of his weight.

NAME ____________________

Lesson 5.5 Figuring Simple Interest

Interest is the amount paid on borrowed money, or amount earned on invested money. **Principal** is the amount borrowed or invested. Use this formula to figure simple interest:

interest = *principal* × *rate* × *time* (in years).

Carla got a $3,000 car loan, to be paid in 2 years. The interest rate is 6%. What will the interest be at the end of the 2 years?

$$i = \$3{,}000 \times 0.06 \times 2 = \$360$$

Toni got a loan for 2 years. The interest rate was 6%. She paid $120 in interest. How much was the principal?

$$120 = p \times 0.06 \times 2 \quad 120 = p \times 0.12$$

$$\frac{120}{0.12} = p \quad \$1{,}000 = p$$

Hector got a $500 loan for $1\frac{1}{2}$ years. He paid $60 interest. What was the interest rate?

$$60 = 500 \times r \times 1.5 \quad 60 = 750r \quad \frac{60}{750} = r$$

$$0.08 = r \quad 8\% = r$$

David got a loan for $1,700. The interest rate was 5%. He paid $212.50 in interest. What was the length of the loan?

$$212.5 = 1{,}700 \times 0.05 \times t$$

$$212.5 = 85t \quad 2.5 = t$$

Fill in the missing information about each loan.

	Principal	Rate	Time	Interest
1.	$5,000	________	3 years	$750
2.	$2,500	3%	________	$112.50
3.	$800	$5\frac{1}{2}$%	4 years	________
4.	________	4%	$2\frac{1}{2}$ years	$650

Solve each problem.

6. Monica got a $4,500 car loan, to be paid in 3 years. The interest rate is 5%. What will the interest be at the end of the 3 years?

   The interest will be $________.

7. Gabriel got a loan for $1\frac{1}{2}$ years. The interest rate was 4%. He paid interest of $240. How much was the principal?

   The principal was $________.

NAME ______________________

Lesson 5.6 Figuring Compound Interest

Compound interest is interest paid on principal and interest already earned.

A savings account earns 3% interest, compounded annually. If the amount in the account is $500 at the start of the loan, how much will be in the account after 4 years?

Year 1: $500 + (500 \times 0.03) = 515$

Year 2: $515 + (515 \times 0.03) = 530.45$

Year 3: $530.45 + (530.45 \times 0.03) = 546.36$

Year 4: $546.36 + (546.36 \times 0.03) = 562.75$

The graph below shows the compounding interest.

$500 with 3% Interest Compounded Annually

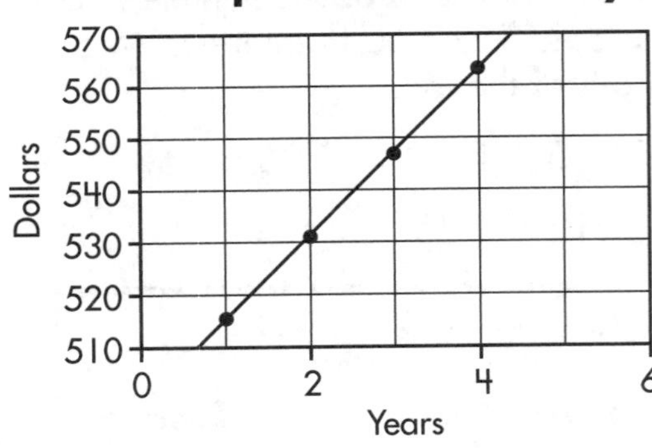

If interest is compounded more than once a year, divide the amount compounded each time by the number of times it is compounded annually.

For interest compounded:	Divide by:
semi-annually	2
quarterly	4
monthly	12

An account of $500 pays 5% compounded monthly. At the end of Month 1, the account will have:
$\$500 + (\$500 \times 0.05 \div 12) = \$502.08$

Find the total amount in each account after the given time. Round to cents.

	Principal	Rate	Time	Compounded	Total Amount
1.	$2,500	8%	4 years	annually	________
2.	$3,000	$5\frac{1}{2}$%	3 years	annually	________
3.	$1,500	$3\frac{1}{2}$%	2 years	semi-annually	________
4.	$700	5%	1 year	quarterly	________

Solve the problem below.

5. Elena has $500 to invest. She can put it in an account that earns 4% compounded semi-annually or in an account that earns 5% simple interest. After 2 years, how much will be in each account, including the principal?

The 4% account will have $________. The 5% account will have $________.

NAME ___________________

Check What You Learned

Proportion, Percent, and Interest

Circle the proportions that are true. Show your work.

	a	b	c
1.	$\frac{3}{2} = \frac{75}{50}$	$\frac{10}{7} = \frac{30}{21}$	$\frac{2}{5} = \frac{4}{15}$
2.	$\frac{2}{4} = \frac{7}{14}$	$\frac{7}{9} = \frac{49}{81}$	$\frac{13}{8} = \frac{39}{24}$

Solve the *n* in each proportion.

3. $\frac{7}{n} = \frac{28}{32}$ ________ $\frac{n}{12} = \frac{120}{144}$ ________ $\frac{25}{50} = \frac{n}{18}$ ________

4. $\frac{7}{21} = \frac{5}{n}$ ________ $\frac{70}{49} = \frac{n}{7}$ ________ $\frac{n}{5} = \frac{8}{40}$ ________

For each fraction or mixed numeral, write the equivalent percent. For each percent, write the equivalent fraction or mixed numeral.

5. 9% = ________ ________% = $1\frac{1}{5}$ 35% = ________

6. ________% = $\frac{19}{20}$ 12% = ________ ________% = $\frac{12}{25}$

For each decimal, write the equivalent percent. For each percent, write the equivalent decimal.

7. 6.07% = ________ ________% = 0.435 59% = ________

8. ________% = 0.098 233% = ________ ________% = 0.0072

CHAPTER 5 POSTTEST

NAME ____________________

Check What You Learned

Proportion, Percent, and Interest

Complete each sentence.

	a	b
9.	35% of 205 is ________.	42 is ________% of 120.
10.	11 is 20% of ________.	________ is 4% more than 50.

Fill in the missing information about each loan.

	Principal	Rate	Time	Compounded	Interest	Total Amount
11.	$6,000	________	4 years	no	$1,200	$7,200
12.	$3,500	4%	________	no	$280	$3,780
13.	$750	3%	5 years	no	________	________
14.	________	6%	$\frac{1}{2}$ year	no	$90	________
15.	$4,000	$3\frac{1}{2}$%	3 years	annually	________	________
16.	$500	8%	2 years	semi-annually	________	________

Solve each problem.

17. Angelina ran 2 miles in 15 minutes. At that rate, how far will she run in 1 hour?

She will run ________ miles.

18. At the end of summer, all sandals are marked down by 70%. If a pair of sandals originally cost $19.50, how much will it cost at the end of summer?

It will cost $________ at the end of summer.

CHAPTER 5 POSTTEST

NAME ______________________

Mid-Test Chapters 1–5

Rewrite each expression using the property indicated.

	a	b
1.	identity: $1 \times p =$ ________	associative: $(9 + k) + 3 =$ ________
2.	commutative: $z \times 7n =$ ________	distributive: $6w + 6x =$ ________

Underline the operation that should be done first. Then, find the value of the equation.

	a	b	c
3.	$9 + 8 \div -4 =$ ________	$4 \times (-6 + 3) + 8 \div 2 =$ ________	$(2 + 6) \times (-4 - 8) =$ ________
4.	$6 + 15 \div 3 \times 2 =$ ________	$(8 - 3) \times 2 \div 8 =$ ________	$4 \times [11 \times (6 - 3)] =$ ________

Solve each equation.

5.	$p + 33 = 105$ ________	$k - 74 = 17$ ________	$14 \times a = 126$ ________
6.	$396 \div b = 99$ ________	$84 - g = 45$ ________	$29 = y + 18$ ________
7.	$0 \div 65n =$ ________	$\frac{m}{6} - 2 = 13$ ________	$31 = 4t + 3$ ________

Write an equation for each problem. Use *n* as the variable. Then, solve the equation.

8. Nick worked 8 hours today and earned a total of $54. What is Nick's hourly wage?

Equation ________________ Nick earns $________ per hour.

9. Jack and Dion sold a total of 33 appliances for their store. Dion sold 3 less than twice as many appliances as Jack sold. How many appliances did each person sell?

Equation ________________ Jack sold ________ and Dion sold ________ appliances.

NAME ______________________

Mid-Test Chapters 1–5

Write the ordered pair for each lettered point. Plot the points for the ordered pairs given.

	a	b	c
10.	*W* ________	*X* ________	*Y* ________
11.	*A* (–2, 3)	*B* (6, –4)	*C* (–5, –3)
12.	*D* (5, 2)	*E* (–8, –6)	*F* (7, –2)

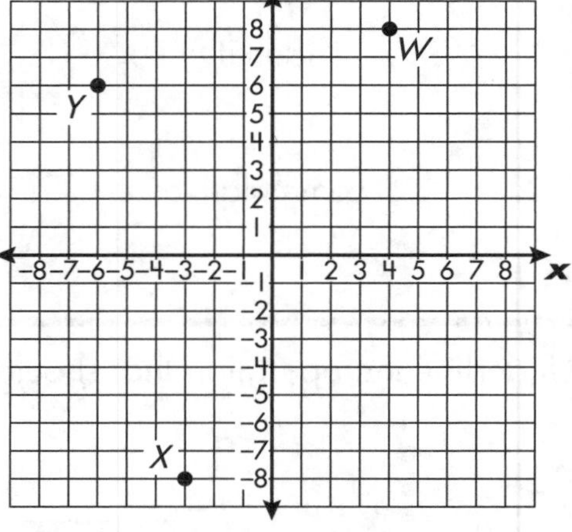

Change each fraction to its simplest form.

	a	b	c
13.	$\frac{18}{42}$ = ____________	$\frac{39}{65}$ = ____________	$\frac{30}{45}$ = ____________
14.	$\frac{12de}{36d}$ = ____________	$\frac{14c^3}{21c}$ = ____________	$\frac{4def}{10d^2e^2}$ = ____________

Solve the following equations.

15.	$6^2 - 2^3$ = ____________	$4^4 + 2^4$ = ____________	$(6 + 3)^2$ = ____________
16.	$5^3 - 25$ = ____________	$(5 - 3)^3$ = ____________	$y + 2^0 = 40$ ____________

Rewrite each expression using a base and an exponent.

17.	$7^{-6} \times 7^3$ = ____________	$4^{-5} \times 4^{-3}$ = ____________	$6^5 \div 6^{-7}$ = ____________

Write each number in scientific notation.

18.	7,564 ____________	0.0897 ____________	32,857 ____________

NAME ______________________

Mid-Test Chapters 1–5

Solve each problem. Write the answer in simplest form.

	a	b	c
19.	$4\frac{2}{3} + 2\frac{11}{12}$	$5\frac{1}{4} - \frac{5}{8}$	$2\frac{1}{9} - 1\frac{2}{3}$
20.	$\frac{3}{8} \times 3\frac{1}{3} =$ ________	$4 \div \frac{2}{5} =$ ________	$2\frac{1}{6} \div 5\frac{1}{4} =$ ________

Solve the following equations. Write each answer in simplest form.

21.	$p + 6.2 = 4.5$ ________	$4y = \frac{1}{2}$ ________	$-3.2b = -12.4$ ________
22.	$m \times \frac{3}{8} = -2$ ________	$k - (-\frac{3}{4}) = \frac{11}{12}$ ________	$-n + \frac{2}{3} = \frac{5}{6}$ ________

Find the next number in each sequence.

	a	b
23.	2.5, 3.75, 5, 6.25, 7.5, ________	1,024, 256, 64, 16, 4, 1, ________

Write an equation for each problem. Use *n* as the variable. Then, solve the equation.

24. To make a trail mix, Terry combined $2\frac{1}{3}$ pounds of peanuts, $\frac{3}{4}$ pound of almonds, and $1\frac{1}{6}$ pounds of cashews. How much trail mix does Terry have?

Equation ________________ Terry has ________ pounds of trail mix.

25. Tamika used $6\frac{1}{4}$ gallons of paint. Each room she painted took $1\frac{1}{4}$ gallons. How many rooms did she paint?

Equation ________________ Tamika painted ________ rooms.

NAME ______________________

Mid-Test Chapters 1–5

Find the value of n in each proportion.

	a	b	c
26.	$\frac{5}{8} = \frac{n}{3}$ ________	$\frac{n}{6} = \frac{44}{3}$ ________	$\frac{3}{16} = \frac{24}{n}$ ________
27.	$\frac{12}{n} = \frac{72}{3}$ ________	$\frac{18}{15} = \frac{n}{5}$ ________	$\frac{30}{n} = \frac{6}{7}$ ________

Complete each sentence.

28. 16 is ________% of 80. 3.5% of 420 is ________.

________ is 6% more than 190.

29. 21 is 25% of ________. 120 is ________% less than 150.

8.2 is ________% of 40.

30. A machine makes 36 widgets in 20 minutes. At that rate, how many widgets will the machine make in an 8-hour day?

The machine will make ________ widgets in a day.

31. A bricklayer had 260 bricks. He used 85% of them to build a wall. How many bricks does he have left?

The bricklayer has ________ bricks left.

Fill in the missing information about each loan.

	Principal	Rate	Time	Compounded	Interest	Total Amount
32.	\$2,000	________	5 years	no	\$1,250.00	\$3,250
33.	\$4,200	$6\frac{1}{4}$ %	________	no	\$2,100	\$6,300
34.	\$6,000	4%	3 years	annually	________	________
35.	\$300	5%	2 years	semi-annually	________	________

NAME ____________________

Check What You Know

Probability and Graphs

Answer the questions by interpreting data from each graph.

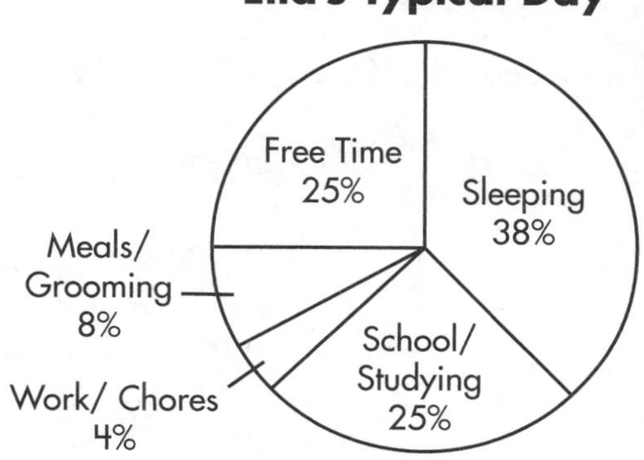

1. How does Ella spend the largest part of her day? ________
2. What percent of her day is free time? ________
3. That percent is represented by how many degrees on the circle graph? ________
4. How many hours per day would that be? ________

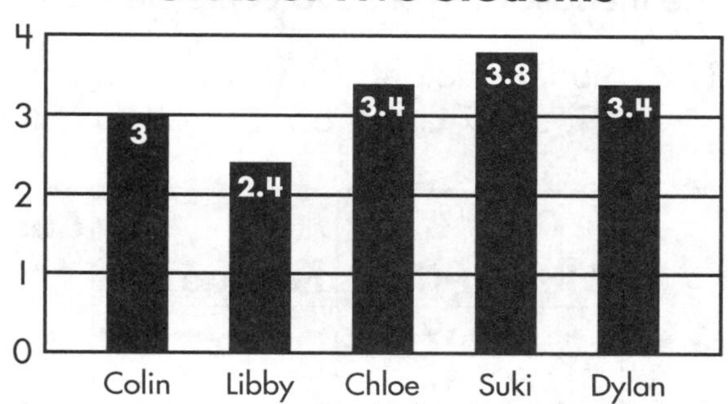

5. Which student has the highest GPA? ________
6. Which two students have the same GPA? ________ and ________
7. How much higher is Chloe's GPA than Libby's? ________
8. Last year, Colin's GPA was 2.8. Has it increased or decreased? ________ By how much? ________

Time Spent Volunteering (Hours per Month)

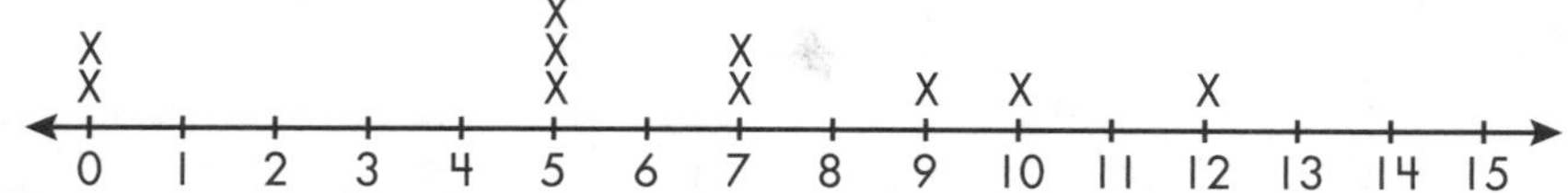

9. How many data points are there? ________
10. What is the mode of the data? ________
11. What is the median of the data? ________
12. What is the mean of the data? ________
13. What is the range of the data? ________

CHAPTER 6 PRETEST

NAME ____________________

Check What You Know

Probability and Graphs

Find the measures of central tendency in each of the following data sets.

14.

a

18, 16, 19, 21, 22, 14, 19, 20, 19, 12

mean: ________

median: ________

mode: ________

range: ________

b

141, 125, 160, 199, 182, 153, 125

mean: ________

median: ________

mode: ________

range: ________

Use the following data to complete the frequency table. Then, answer the questions.

15. Student Heights (in inches): 62, 64, 58, 66, 67, 62, 67, 70, 60, 58, 59, 59, 61, 65, 65, 68, 69, 58, 71, 68, 65, 64, 64, 59, 63, 63, 72, 62, 61, 61, 65

Height (in.)	Frequency	Cumulative Frequency	Relative Frequency	
			As Fraction	As Percent
58–59				
60–61				
62–63				
64–65				
66–67				
68–69				
70–71				
72–73				

16. In which height range are the largest percent of students? ________

17. How many students are 70 in. or taller? ________ What percent is this? ________

Write each answer as a fraction in simplest form.

18. You have six pennies in your pocket. Two are from the year 2001, 2 from 1996, 1 from 1982, and 1 from 1972. What is the probability of drawing a penny from 2001? ________

19. What is the probability of drawing a penny from either 2001 or 1972? ________

NAME ______________________

Lesson 6.1 Calculating

Probability is the likelihood that a given event will happen. To find probability, compare the number of ways a given event can occur to the total number of possible outcomes (also called the **sample space**). If the outcomes are equally likely, the probability of an event occurring is the number of ways the event (E) can occur divided by the number of possible outcomes in the sample space (S), or $P(E) = \frac{n(E)}{n(S)}$. For example, the probability of rolling a 2 on a single roll of a die is $\frac{1}{6}$ because there is only one way to roll a 2 out of the six ways the die could be rolled.

A **compound event** consists of two simple events. Tossing a die is a simple event. Tossing two dice is a compound event. Events are *independent* when the outcome of one event does not influence the outcome of the second event. Events are *dependent* when the outcome of one event affects the outcome of the second event.

- To find the probability of two independent events both occurring, multiply the probability of the first event (A) by the probability of the second event (B), or $P(A \text{ and } B) = P(A) \times P(B)$.
- To find the probability of two dependent events both occurring, multiply the probability of A by the probability of B after A occurs, or $P(A \text{ and } B) = P(A) \times P(B \text{ following } A)$.
- To find the probability of one or the other of two events occurring, add the probability of the first event to the probability of the second event, or $P(A \text{ or } B) = P(A) + P(B)$.

Write each answer as a fraction in simplest form.

1. You roll a standard six-sided die. What is the probability that you roll a 6? ________

2. You roll the die again. What is the probability that you roll a multiple of 3? ________

3. You roll twice. What is the probability that you roll a 6 both times? ________

4. You have 4 marbles in your pocket: 1 red, 1 blue, 1 black, and 1 white. You pull a marble out of your pocket. What is the probability that you pull out a red marble? ________

5. What is the probability that you pull out either a blue marble or a black marble?

   The probability is ________.

NAME ______________________

Lesson 6.2 Frequency Tables

Frequency is how often an item, a number, or a range of numbers occurs. The **cumulative frequency** is the sum of all frequencies up to and including the current one. The **relative frequency** is the ratio of a specific frequency to the total number of items.

The frequency table below shows the frequencies for these test scores: 71, 85, 73, 92, 86, 79, 87, 98, 82, 93, 81, 89, 88, 96:

Score	Frequency	Cumulative Frequency	Relative Frequency	
			As Fraction	As Percent
71–75	2	2	$\frac{2}{14}$ or $\frac{1}{7}$	(14.3%)
76–80	1	3	$\frac{1}{14}$	(7.1%)
81–85	3	6	$\frac{3}{14}$	(21.4%)
86–90	4	10	$\frac{4}{14}$ or $\frac{2}{7}$	(28.6%)
91–95	2	12	$\frac{2}{14}$ or $\frac{1}{7}$	(14.3%)
96–100	2	14	$\frac{2}{14}$ or $\frac{1}{7}$	(14.3%)

The table shows that the scores ranged between 71 and 100, with the greatest number of students scoring between 86 and 90.

Use the following data to complete the frequency table. Then, answer the questions.

1. Daily High Temperatures in March: 40, 43, 38, 44, 48, 48, 56, 60, 61, 72, 65, 56, 50, 48, 47, 61, 63, 66, 67, 69, 54, 45, 61, 65, 55, 46, 59, 51, 55, 62, 79

Temperature	Frequency	Cumulative Frequency	Relative Frequency	
			As Fraction	As Percent
35–40				
41–45				
46–50				
51–55				
56–60				
61–65				
66–70				
71–75				
76–80				

2. How many days had high temperatures of 40 or lower? ________

3. What percent of days had high temperatures between 51 and 60? ________

NAME ______________________________

Lesson 6.3 Measures of Central Tendency

Measures of central tendency are numbers used to represent a set of data. Three types of measures of central tendency are the mean, median, and mode. The **mean** is the average of a set of numbers. To find the mean, add all the numbers and divide by the number of items in the data set. The **median** is the middle number of a set of numbers that is ordered from least to greatest. If there are two middle numbers, the median is the mean of the two. The **mode** is the number that appears most often in a set of numbers. There is no mode if all numbers appear the same number of times. The **range** is the difference between the greatest and least numbers in the data set. The **interquartile range** is the difference between the greatest and least numbers in the middle 50% of the data set.

Scores on Final Exam			
Student A	84	Student F	88
Student B	80	Student G	86
Student C	78	Student H	80
Student D	90	Student I	94
Student E	76	Student J	74

First, arrange the numbers from least to greatest:

74, 76, 78, 80, <u>80, 84</u>, 86, 88, 90, 94

Median = $\frac{(80 + 84)}{2} = 82$

Mode = 80 (number that appears most often)

Range = 94 − 74 = 20

Mean = $\frac{(84 + 80 + 78 + 90 + 76 + 88 + 86 + 80 + 94 + 74)}{10} = \frac{830}{10} = 83$

1. Find the measures of central tendency for each of the following data sets.

a

41, 50, 68, 67, 45, 68, 60

mean: ________ median: ________

mode: ________ range: ________

b

73, 69, 67, 80, 65, 78, 75, 69

mean: ________ median: ________

mode: ________ range: ________

2. Find the measures of central tendency for the data in the graph below.

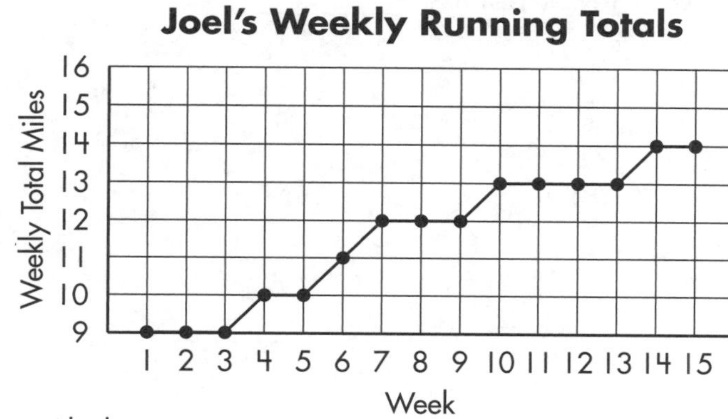

mean: ________

median: ________

mode: ________

range: ________

NAME ____________________

Lesson 6.4 Line Plots

A **line plot** uses a number line to clearly illustrate the frequency of data. Each data point is indicated by an X on the number line.

Jin made this line plot:

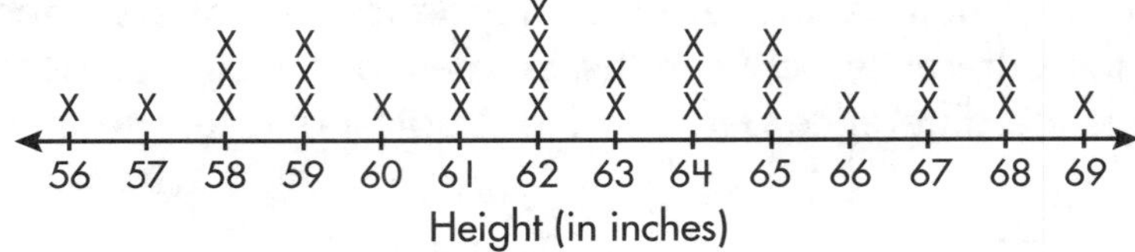

What is the mode, or most frequent height? Look for the tallest stack of Xs. The mode is 62 inches.

What is the range of heights in the class? Subtract the least height from the greatest:
69 – 56 = 13 inches

What is the median height of the students? Count 15 Xs (half of the total) in from the left and 15 Xs in from the right. The median is the average of these two numbers. Because both numbers are 62 inches, the median is 62 inches.

What is the mean height of the students? Add all of the heights and divide by the total number of Xs: 56 + 57 + 58(3) + 59(3) + 60 + 61(3) + 62(4) + 63(2) + 64(3) + 65(3) + 66 + 67(2) + 68(2) + 69 = 1873 ÷ 30 = 62.43

Interpret the line plot below to answer the questions that follow.

Basketball Team Scores

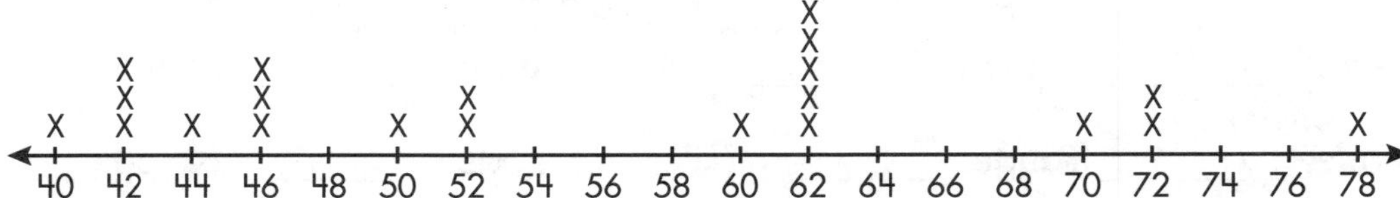

1. In how many games did the team score 70 or more points? ________
2. In how many games did the team score 50 or fewer points? ________
3. How many data points are there? ________
4. What is the mode of the data? ________
5. What is the median of the data? ________
6. What is the mean of the data? ________
7. What is the range of the data? ________

NAME ______________________

Lesson 6.5 Bar and Line

Bar graphs are used to compare data. This graph shows the results of an eighth grade poll that asked, "What is your favorite type of music?"

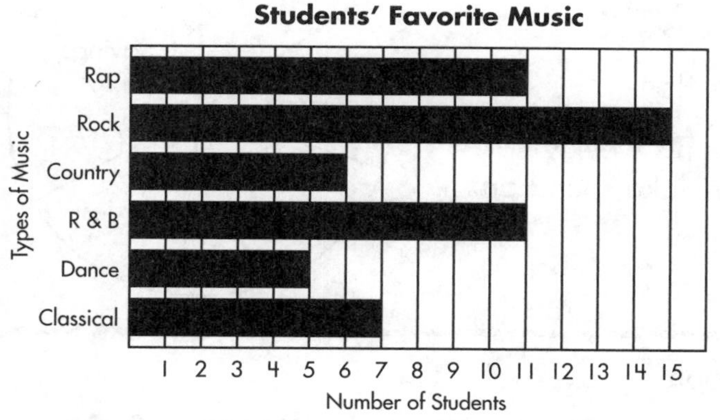

Which type of music did most students pick? Rock. How many students chose either country or dance music? 5 + 6 = 11

Line graphs show how data changes over time. This line graph shows temperature changes during two weeks in May.

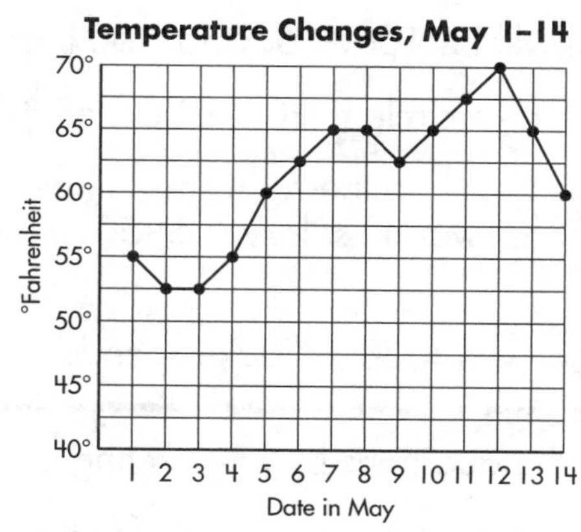

What was the range of temperatures? 70 – 52.5 = 17.5

Answer the questions below by interpreting data from the bar graph.

1. Which type of music did the fewest students pick? ________
2. How many students chose rap music? ________
3. How many total students were polled? ________
4. What percent of students chose rap music? ________

Answer the questions below by interpreting data from the line graph.

5. What was the mean temperature from May 1 to May 14? ________
6. What was the median temperature from May 1 to May 14? ________
7. What was the mode, or most frequent temperature? ________
8. If the graph ended with May 13, which would change: the mean, the median, or the mode?

____

NAME ___________________________

Lesson 6.6 Circle Graph

A **circle graph** is used to show how a whole is divided. The entire circle represents 1 whole. It is divided into sectors, which are fractional parts of the whole. A circle graph can be divided into any number of segments of any percentage or fraction value.

The total will be 100%, or 360°. 50% or $\frac{1}{2}$ of a circle is 180°.

25% or $\frac{1}{4}$ of a circle is 90°. 12.5% or $\frac{1}{8}$ of a circle is 45°.

The circle graph to the right shows how Jake spends his weekly salary. If his weekly salary is $450, how much does Jake spend on pizza?

$\frac{24}{360} = \frac{x}{450}$ $x = 30$ Jake spends $30.

Answer the questions by interpreting each circle graph.

1. What category accounted for the greatest amount of waste in 2008? ________
2. What percent of the total waste was this? ________
3. 250 million tons of waste were generated in 2008. How many tons were paper? ________
4. How many tons were yard trimmings and food scraps? ________

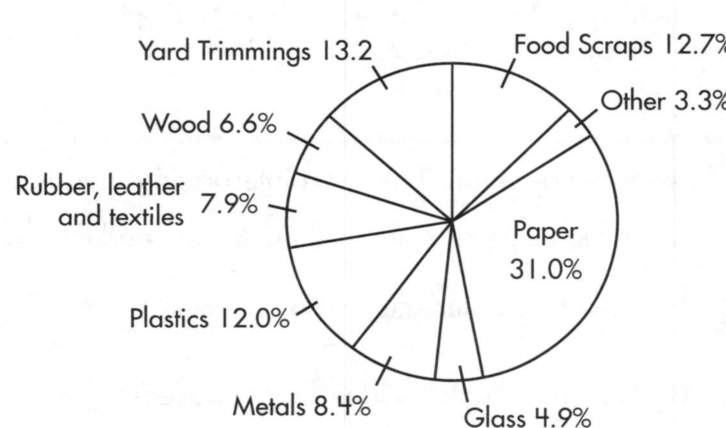

5. What percent of the population was less than 20 years old? ________
6. What percent of the population was 65 or older? ________
7. That percent is represented by how many degrees on the circle graph? ________
8. The total population of the United States in 2000 was 281,421,906. About how many people were between the ages of 20 and 44? ________

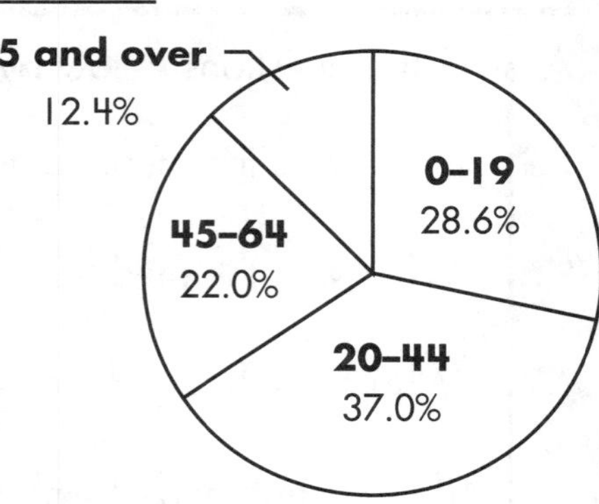

NAME ___________________________

Check What You Learned

Probability and Graphs

CHAPTER 6 POSTTEST

Answer the questions by interpreting data from each graph.

How Elena Uses Her Allowance

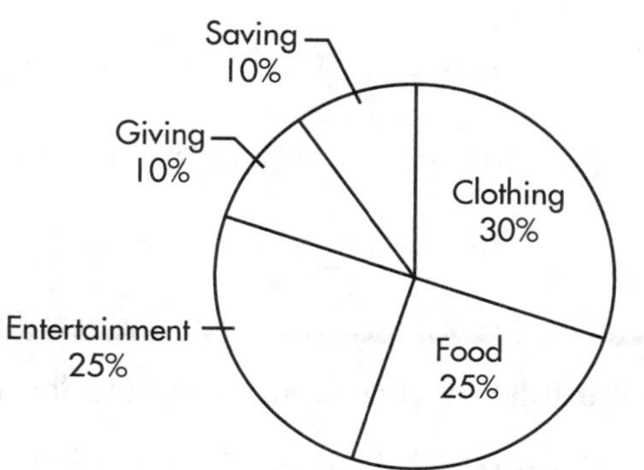

1. On what does Elena spend the largest part of her allowance? ________

2. What percent of her allowance is spent on entertainment? ________

3. That percent is represented by how many degrees on the circle graph? ________

4. If Elena's allowance is $20 per week, how much does she save each week? ________

Tornadoes in May, 1995–2000

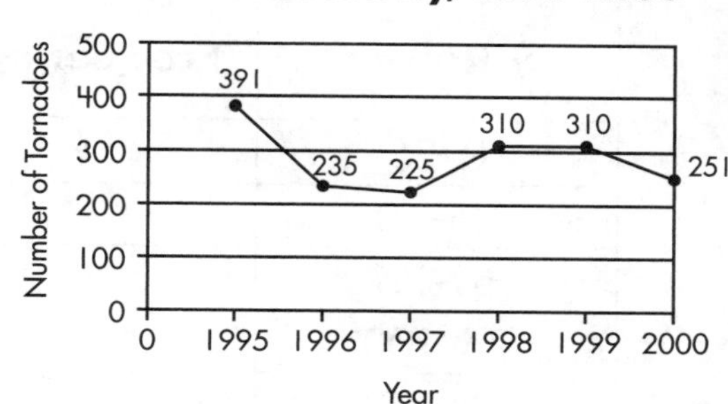

5. In which year did the most tornadoes occur? ________ The fewest? ________

6. What was the mean number of tornadoes during this period? ________

7. In which two years did the same number of tornadoes occur? ________ Is this the median or the mode of the data? ________

Hours of Exercise Per Week

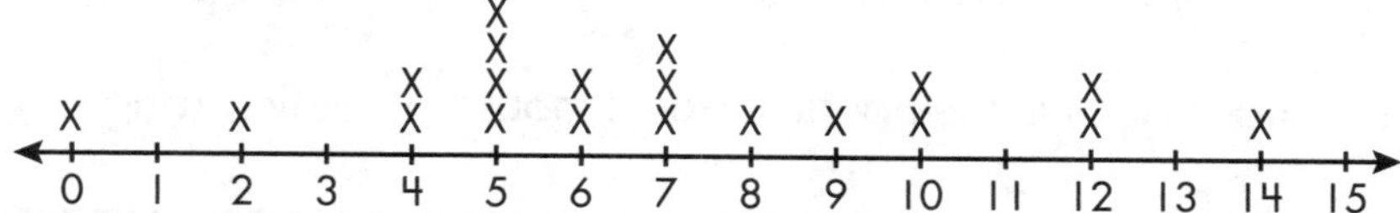

8. What is the mode of the data? ________

9. What is the median of the data? ________

10. What is the mean of the data? ________

NAME ________________

Check What You Learned

Probability and Graphs

11. Find the measures of central tendency in each of the following data sets.

a	b
57, 70, 87, 93, 54, 69, 57	125, 136, 118, 154, 127, 142, 157, 154
mean: ________ median: ________	mean: ________ median: ________
mode: ________ range: ________	mode: ________ range: ________

Use the following data to complete the frequency table. Then, answer the questions.

12. Amounts Raised by Each Club Member: $25, $30, $50, $50, $100, $35, $15, $120, $180, $80, $155, $170, $80, $60, $75, $105, $125, $90, $40, $130

$ Raised	Frequency	Cumulative Frequency	Relative Frequency	
			As Fraction	As Percent
0–25				
26–50				
51–75				
76–100				
101–125				
126–150				
151–175				
176–200				

13. How many club members raised over $100? ________ What percent is this? ________

14. The greatest number of club members raised amounts in which range? ________

Write each answer as a fraction in simplest form.

15. There are 52 cards in a deck and 4 suits (spades, clubs, hearts, and diamonds). Each suit has 1 jack, 1 queen, and 1 king. What is the probability of drawing a king of any suit?

____

16. What is the probability of drawing a king or a queen? ________

Check What You Know

Equations and Inequalities

Solve each equation. Write *null* if the equation has no solution. Write *all* if all numbers solve the equation. Write fractions in simplest form.

	a	b
1.	$15 + n = 2n$ ________	$7 - p = 3p + 5$ ________
2.	$6y + 2 = 4y$ ________	$0.6x = 2.2x - 4$ ________
3.	$\frac{2r}{3} = 10 - r$ ________	$3(m + 2) = 21$ ________
4.	$14 = 2(n - 3) + 6$ ________	$5(b + 4) = 5(b + 6) - 10$ ________
5.	$4(z - 1) = 3(z + 2)$ ________	$7(a + 3) = 7a + 11$ ________

Write $<$, $>$, or $=$ on the line to compare the values.

	a	b	c
6.	25 ________ 14	−1 ________ 0	$\frac{1}{4}$ ________ 0.3
7.	15% ________ 0.15	$\frac{5}{8}$ ________ 61%	−5 ________ −3

Write $\leq$ or $\geq$ on the line to complete the inequality.

8. Carmen will make at least $30 doing chores. Carmen's earnings will be ________ $30.

9. To lose weight, Brad wants to consume no more than 2,000 calories a day. Brad wants his daily consumption to be ________ 2,000 calories.

NAME ____________________

Check What You Know

Equations and Inequalities

Solve each inequality. Write the solution with the variable on the left side.

	a	b	c
10.	$n + 7 < 10$ ______	$a - 14 > 8$ ______	$16 \leq 10 + p$ ______
11.	$w + 6 \geq -3$ ______	$-8 < m - 5$ ______	$9x > 27$ ______
12.	$\frac{b}{7} < 6$ ______	$-3c \leq 9$ ______	$\frac{k}{-8} < 4$ ______
13.	$-8 \geq -4y$ ______	$5 < \frac{p}{2}$ ______	$4n + 5 < 29$ ______
14.	$7 \leq 8r - 1$ ______	$-5d + 7 \geq 42$ ______	$-10 < -4x + 2$ ______
15.	$\frac{y}{6} + 3 > 4$ ______	$19\% \leq 3x + 4\%$ ______	$12.4 < 3.9 - 5k$ ______

Write an inequality for each problem. Use n as the variable. Then, solve the inequality. Include the proper inequality symbol in the solution.

16. An auto mechanic estimates that the cost to repair Brett's car will be no more than \$200. The parts will cost \$49.23. What is the estimated cost for the labor?

Inequality: ________ Solution: ________________

17. Tawana has \$325.54 in her checking account. She must keep a balance of at least \$300 to avoid a fee. She plans to write a check to pay her credit card bill of \$125.43. How much money must Tawana deposit in her account to maintain at least the minimum balance?

Inequality: ________ Solution: ________________

NAME ______________________

Lesson 7.1 Equations with Variables on Each Side

Sometimes a variable appears on both sides of an equation. When this happens, use the properties of equality to rewrite the equation with the variable on the one side. Then, solve.

$4 + 3x = 5x$	
$4 + 3x - 3x = 5x - 3x$	Subtraction Property
$4 = 2x$	Simplify
$\frac{4}{2} = \frac{2x}{2}$	Division Property
$2 = x$	Solution

$2n = -4n - 3$	
$2n + 4n = -4n - 3 + 4n$	Addition Property
$6n = -3$	Simplify
$\frac{6n}{6} = \frac{-3}{6}$	Division Property
$n = \frac{-1}{2}$	Solution

Solve each equation. Write fractions in simplest form.

	a	b	c
1.	$8b + 2 = 10b$ ________	$15 + c = 2c - 5$ ________	$30x + 3 = 10 - 5x$ ________
2.	$7t + 2t = t - 6$ ________	$28 + p = 15p$ ________	$0.23n = 2.73n - 5$ ________
3.	$6a + 9 = 3a$ ________	$1.4x - 8 = x + 12$ ________	$4m + 24 = 36 + m$ ________
4.	$-2d = 4d - 42$ ________	$\frac{8g}{4} = g + 9$ ________	$2r = 4r - 14.2$ ________

Write an equation for each statement, using x for the variable. Then, solve the equation.

5. Three times a number plus 5 equals 10 more than the same number.

Equation: ________________ Solution: ________

6. Six more than half of a number equals the same number times 2.

Equation: ________________ Solution: ________

NAME ________________________

Lesson 7.2 Equations with Grouping Symbols

To solve equations with grouping symbols, such as parentheses, first use the distributive property to remove the parentheses. Then, solve.

Solve: $3(2 + n) = 10 + 2n$		$6 + n = 10$	Simplify
$(3 \times 2) + (3 \times n) = 10 + 2n$	Distributive Property	$6 + n - 6 = 10 - 6$	Subtraction Property
$6 + 3n = 10 + 2n$	Simplify	$n = 4$	Solution
$6 + 3n - 2n = 10 + 2n - 2n$	Subtraction Property		

Some equations have no solutions. The symbol ∅ means **null**, or no solution. Some equations have an infinite number of solutions, or true for all solutions.

$2 + a = 4 + a$

$2 + a - a = 4 + a - a$

$2 = 4$

This equation is never true. Therefore, the solution is ∅ (null).

$10b - 5 = 2(5b - 2) - 1$

$10b - 5 = 10b - 4 - 1$

$10b - 5 = 10b - 5$

$10b = 10b$ after adding 5 to each side

$b = b$ after dividing each side by 10

This equation is always true. Therefore, the solution is true for all numbers.

Solve the equations. Write *null* or *all* where appropriate. Show fractions in simplest form.

	a	b
1.	$5(y + 2) = 20$ ________	$16 = 4(n - 5) + 4$ ________
2.	$2(x - 4) = 2x - 8$ ________	$7p + 9 = 4(p - 3)$ ________
3.	$6(k + 3) = 2(4k + 5)$ ________	$3(2m + 4) = 6m + 15$ ________
4.	$30 - 2x = 2(3x + 3)$ ________	$2(4w + 7) = 3(6 + 2w)$ ________
5.	$6(2 + 3z) = 3(4 + 6z)$ ________	$25 = 6(c + 7) - 14$ ________
6.	$4g + 9 = 2(g - 6) + 2g$ ________	$3(3h + h) = 2(h + 5)$ ________

NAME ____________________

Lesson 7.3 Inequalities

Recall that the = symbol means *equal to*. This symbol indicates an equation, or equality. An **inequality** states that values are not equal. The symbols $>$ and $<$ indicate inequality. Sometimes the values in an inequality might also be equal. For example, a tank holds 15 gallons of gas. How much gas is in the tank? You don't know without measuring. However, you do know that the amount must be less than or equal to 15 gallons: Gas in tank $\leq$ 15 gallons.

Symbol	Meaning
$>$	greater than
$<$	less than
$\geq$	greater than or equal to
$\leq$	less than or equal to

You can use inequality symbols to compare percents, fractions, and decimals. First, express the numbers in the same format so they are easier to compare.

$\frac{1}{5}$ ________ 30%		0.45 ________ 38%
20% ________ 30%	Convert 1 of the numbers.	45% ________ 38%
20% ___$<$___ 30%	Compare the numbers.	45% ___$>$___ 38%

Write >, <, or = on the line to compare the given values.

	a	b	c
1.	40% ________ $\frac{1}{5}$	0.25 ________ $\frac{1}{6}$	$\frac{1}{8}$ ________ 0.15
2.	94% ________ 0.89	12% ________ 12	$\frac{3}{4}$ ________ 0.85
3.	$\frac{5}{8}$ ________ 62.5%	0.05 ________ $\frac{1}{9}$	514% ________ 5.14
4.	$21\frac{1}{7}$ ________ 21.19	23.5 ________ 235%	30% ________ $\frac{3}{100}$

Write $\geq$ or $\leq$ on the line to complete the inequality.

5. In 1 year, Lana wants to save at least \$500. Lana wants her savings to be ________ \$500.

6. Jordan takes \$20 to the mall. Using cash only, Jordan will spend ________ \$20.

NAME ______________________

Lesson 7.4 Solving Inequalities by Adding or Subtracting

The Addition and Subtraction Properties also apply to inequalities. You can add or subtract the same number from both sides of an inequality without affecting the inequality.

Solve: $n + 4 < 9$ $\quad n + 4 - 4 < 9 - 4$ $\quad n < 5$

The solution is that n can be any value less than 5.

If you swap the left side and right side of an inequality, you must reverse the direction of the inequality. The direction is the way the arrow points.

$n < 5$	$x - 6 > 3$	$p \leq 9$	$k - 7 \geq 6$
$5 > n$	$3 < x - 6$	$9 \geq p$	$6 \leq k - 7$
$<$ becomes $>$	$>$ becomes $<$	$\leq$ becomes $\geq$	$\geq$ becomes $\leq$

Solve each inequality. Show the solution with the variable on the left side.

	a	b	c
1.	$x + 5 > 8$ ________	$t - 4 < 11$ ________	$12 < m + 6$ ________
2.	$y - 3 \leq 7$ ________	$9 + r \geq 5$ ________	$15 \geq 7 + n$ ________
3.	$p + 1 < -5$ ________	$z + 3 + 5 < 28$ ________	$-4 \leq w + 12$ ________
4.	$x - 6 \geq 8$ ________	$p + 4 \leq 35$ ________	$22 \geq y + 5 - 7$ ________

Write an inequality for each problem. Use n as the variable. Then, solve the inequality. Include the proper inequality symbol in the solution.

5. Jermaine has $25. He wants to buy a pair of gloves that costs $16.50. He also wants to buy a sandwich. How much can Jermaine spend on the sandwich?

Inequality: ______________________ Solution: ______________

6. Sharon has jogged 1.25 miles. Her goal is to jog more than 3.5 miles. How much more must she jog to accomplish her goal?

Inequality: ______________________ Solution: ______________

NAME ____________________

Lesson 7.5 Solving Inequalities by Multiplying or Dividing

Multiplication and Division Properties also apply to inequalities. You can multiply or divide both sides of an inequality by the same positive number without affecting the inequality. But if you multiply or divide both sides by a negative number, you must reverse the direction of the inequality.

Solve: $4x > 12$	Solve: $\frac{n}{2} \leq 8$	Solve: $-3p < 6$
$\frac{4x}{4} > \frac{12}{4}$	$\frac{n}{2} \times 2 \leq 8 \times 2$	$\frac{-3p}{-3} > \frac{-6}{-3}$ reverse the inequality
$x > 3$	$n \leq 16$	$p > -2$

Remember to reverse the direction of the inequality if you swap the left and the right sides.

Solve each inequality. Show the solution with the variable on the left side.

	a	b	c
1.	$5y < 15$ ________	$\frac{k}{6} > 7$ ________	$12 \leq 4n$ ________
2.	$-7h > 28$ ________	$\frac{m}{-4} < 5$ ________	$\frac{c}{6} \geq -2$ ________
3.	$-9p > -18$ ________	$9 \leq \frac{n}{3}$ ________	$30 < 3a$ ________
4.	$4 < -4n$ ________	$2 \leq \frac{b}{-3}$ ________	$2.5x > 40$ ________

Write an inequality for each problem. Use n as the variable. Then, solve the inequality. Include the proper inequality symbol in the solution.

5. Kevin has $26 and wants to rent a bicycle. The bicycle rents for $6.25 per hour. How many hours can Kevin ride without owing more money than he has?

Inequality: ____________________ Solution: ____________

6. Shia wants to save the same amount each month. In 4 months, she wants savings of at least $200. How much money must Shia save each month to achieve her goal?

Inequality: ____________________ Solution: ____________

NAME ______________________

Lesson 7.6 Solving Multi-Step Inequalities

Some problems with inequalities require more than one step to solve. Use the properties of equality to solve the inequality. Remember to reverse the direction of the inequality if you multiply or divide by a negative number or if you swap the sides of the inequality.

$4n + 6 < 18$		$6 - 2n \geq 24$	
$4n + 6 - 6 < 18 - 6$	Subtraction Property	$6 - 2n - 6 \geq 24 - 6$	Subtraction Property
$4n < 12$	Simplify	$-2n \geq 18$	Simplify
$\frac{4n}{4} < \frac{12}{4}$	Division Property	$\frac{-2n}{-2} \leq \frac{18}{-2}$	Reverse direction
$n < 3$	Solution	$n \leq -9$	Solution

Solve each inequality. Show the solution with the variable on the left side.

	a	b	c
1.	$3p + 5 > 26$ ________	$14 \leq 3k - 1$ ________	$-6x + 4 < 40$ ________
2.	$\frac{3z}{5} \geq 9$ ________	$-r + 10 > 20$ ________	$3 + 2b \geq b + 1$ ________
3.	$30 < 7n + 2$ ________	$\frac{4m}{-3} \leq 12$ ________	$3.75 > 2 + 5w$ ________
4.	$5y - 0.25 < 6$ ________	$-2b + 6 \geq 32$ ________	$16\% < 7\% - 3a$ ________

Write an inequality for each problem. Use n as the variable. Then, solve the inequality.

5. Josh wants to download music online. He must buy a membership for $14. Then, he can download songs for 99 cents each. Josh has $20. How many songs can Josh buy without spending more money than he has?

Inequality: ______________________ Solution: ________________

6. Kendra makes $8 per hour mowing lawns in the summer. Gas for the mower costs $16 and will last all summer. How many hours must Kendra mow to earn at least $200?

Inequality: ______________________ Solution: ________________

NAME ______________________

Check What You Learned

Equations and Inequalities

Solve each equation. Write *null* if the equation has no solution. Write *all* if all numbers solve the equation. Write fractions in simplest form.

	a	b
1.	$33 + a = 12a$ ________	$-6n + 2 = 4n - 5$ ________
2.	$2.4b - 7 = b + 15.4$ ________	$\frac{4m}{6} = m + 3$ ________
3.	$4p + \frac{1}{4} = 6p$ ________	$24 - c = 2(3 + 4c)$ ________
4.	$3(5 - 2y) = 4(y + 2)$ ________	$5(2x + 3) = 3(x + 2) + 7x + 9$ ________
5.	$4(3k + 6) = 12(5 + k)$ ________	$3(2n + 4) = 2n + 56$ ________

Write <, >, or = on the line to compare the values.

	a	b	c
6.	53 ________ 85	0.33 ________ 3.4%	$\frac{3}{5}$ ________ 60%
7.	$5\frac{1}{4}$ ________ 520%	−15 ________ −12	−0.8 ________ −75%

Write ≤ or ≥ on the line to complete the inequality.

8. A polling company needs at least 250 responses for its survey to be valid. The number of responses must be ________ 250.

9. If Rima can sign up 10 people or more to attend a concert, everyone will get a discount on the ticket price. Rima needs a group that is ________ 10.

NAME ____________________

Check What You Learned

Equations and Inequalities

Solve each inequality. Write the solution with the variable on the left side.

	a	b	c
10.	$b - 9 < 18$ ________	$11 + k > 24$ ________	$23 < 7 + p$ ________
11.	$-3 \geq n - 8$ ________	$\frac{y}{3} < 12$ ________	$10x \geq 35$ ________
12.	$-3a > -21$ ________	$\frac{c}{-2} \geq 6$ ________	$88 \leq 4t$ ________
13.	$6 > -2d$ ________	$-8 < \frac{g}{-2}$ ________	$4y + 8 < 20$ ________
14.	$12 \leq 7x - 2$ ________	$\frac{3n}{4} \geq 12$ ________	$45 > 11k + 1$ ________
15.	$2.5 < 2 + 5p$ ________	$6\% + 4a \leq 90\%$ ________	$21 < 9 - 6b$ ________

Write an inequality for each problem. Use *n* as the variable. Then, solve the inequality. Include the proper inequality symbol in the solution.

16. Hajime wants to advertise the class carwash in the local newspaper. He can spend no more than \$35 on the advertisement. The newspaper charges 85 cents per word. How many words can Hajime have in the ad?

Inequality: ____________________ Solution: ________________

17. Silvia has a bucket that holds 4.5 quarts of liquid. She put 1.25 quarts of water in the bucket. How much more water can she add without exceeding the amount the bucket can hold?

Inequality: ____________________ Solution: ________________

NAME ______________________

Check What You Know

Functions and Graphing

CHAPTER 8 PRETEST

Complete the function table for each function. Then, graph the function.

1. **a** $y = x - 4$

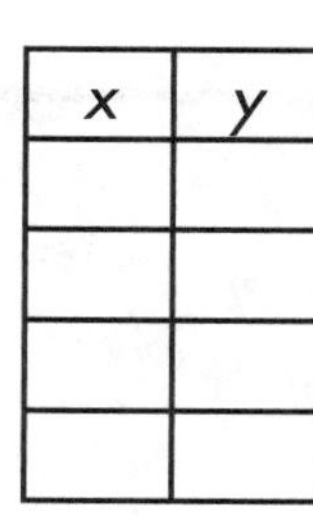

x	y

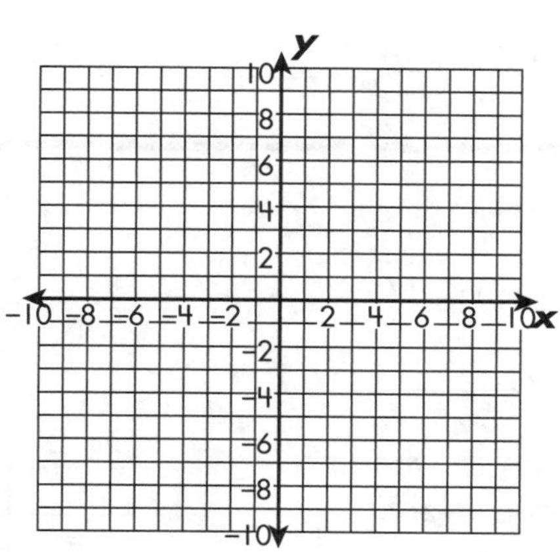

b $y = 3x + 1$

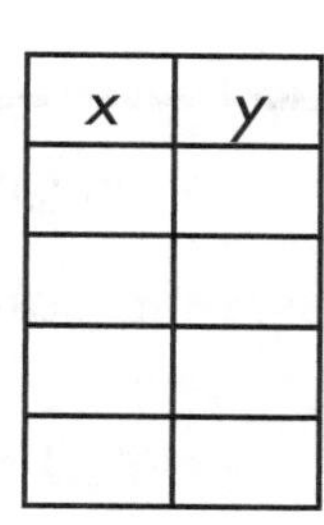

x	y

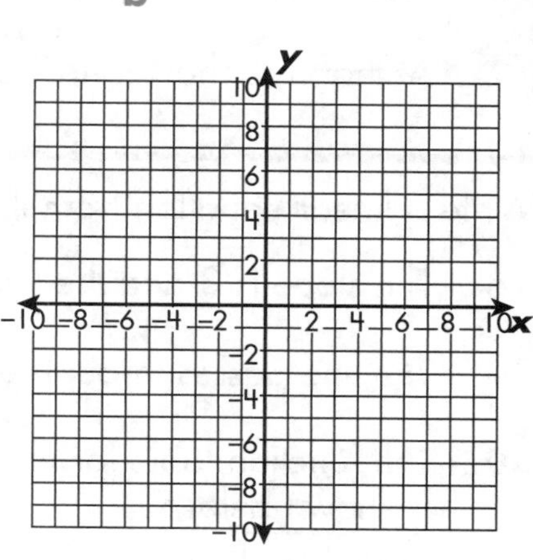

Graph the solution to each inequality.

2. **a** $y > x - 2$

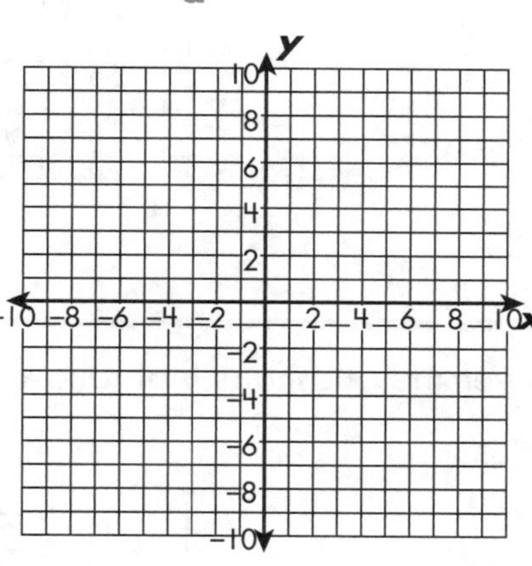

b $y \leq 3x + 2$

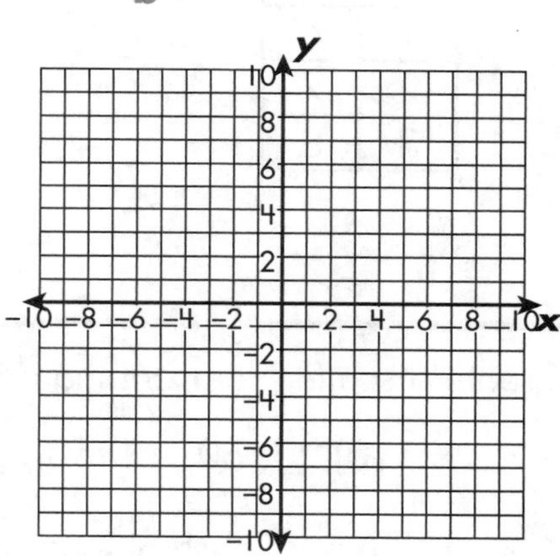

Answer each question.

3. If y varies directly with x and you know that $y = 42$ when $x = 7$, what is the constant of variation? ________

4. If you know that the direct variation equation is $y = 5x$ and $y = 15$, what is x? ________

5. Using the same equation, what is y if $x = 8$? ________

NAME ___________________________

Check What You Know

Functions and Graphing

6. Nicole ran 2 miles in 15 minutes. Express her rate of speed as a direct variation equation, using d for distance and t for time (in minutes). ________

7. At that rate, how long would it take her to run 6 miles? ________

Write a linear equation from the information given below.

8. The slope is 3 and the line passes through point (5, 17). ________

9. The line passes through points (4, 5) and (6, 9). ________

10. The function table for the line is shown below.

x	y
−2	3
−1	4
0	5
1	6
2	7
3	8

____

11. The graph for the line is shown at right.

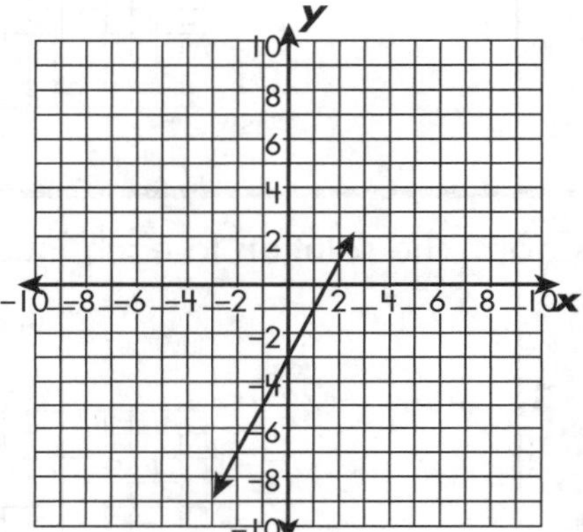

____

Create a scatterplot from the data below. Then, answer the questions that follow.

12. (2, 10), (3, 30), (4, 50), (5, 70), (6, 90), (7, 100)

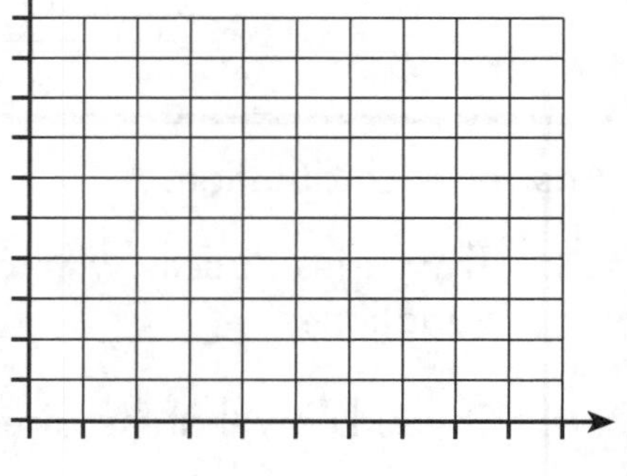

13. Is the relationship linear or nonlinear? ________

14. Is the correlation positive or negative? ________

15. Suppose you learn that the data sets being compared are the number of hours during a marathon (x) and the percentage of people who have completed the marathon (y). Describe the relationship between the two sets of data by completing the sentence below.

As the number of hours ________, the percentage of people who have completed the marathon ________________.

NAME ____________________

Lesson 8.1 Functions and Function Tables

A **function** is a rule for how two variables relate. For each value of x (the domain), there is only one value of y (the range). For example, if $y = x + 6$, whatever x is, y must be greater than x by the number 6.

A **function table** shows the values for each pair of variables as the result of the particular function. A function table for the equation $y = x + 6$ is shown here.

x	y
−1	5
0	6
1	7
2	8
3	9
4	10

Complete each function table for the given functions.

1.

a $y = x - 3$

x	y
0	
1	
2	
3	
4	
5	

b $y = 4x + 2$

x	y
−2	
−1	
0	
1	
2	
3	

c $y = 3x - 1$

x	y
−3	
−2	
−1	
0	
1	
2	

2.

a $y = \frac{x}{2}$

x	y
−2	
0	
2	
4	
6	
8	

b $y = \frac{x}{4} + 2$

x	y
−8	
−4	
0	
4	
8	
12	

c $y = \frac{x}{3} - 1$

x	y
−9	
−6	
−3	
0	
3	
6	

3.

a $y = x^2 + 5$

x	y
0	
1	
2	
3	
4	
5	

b $y = 2x^2 - 1$

x	y
0	
1	
2	
3	
4	
5	

c $y = (x + 1) \div 2$

x	y
−5	
−3	
−1	
1	
3	
5	

NAME ____________________

Lesson 8.2 Graphing Linear Equations

A **linear equation** is an equation that creates a straight line when graphed on a coordinate plane. To graph a linear equation, create a function table with at least 3 ordered pairs. Then, plot these ordered pairs on a coordinate plane. Draw a line through the points. Some points for this linear equation are in the table to the right:

$$y = \frac{x}{2} + 1$$

These points are plotted on the line graph at the right.

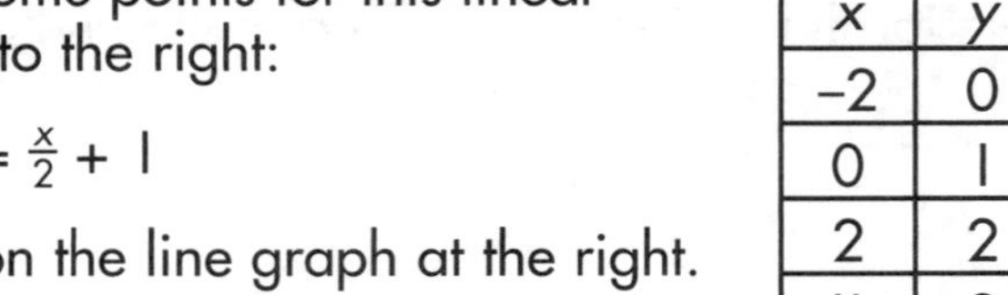

x	y
−2	0
0	1
2	2
4	3

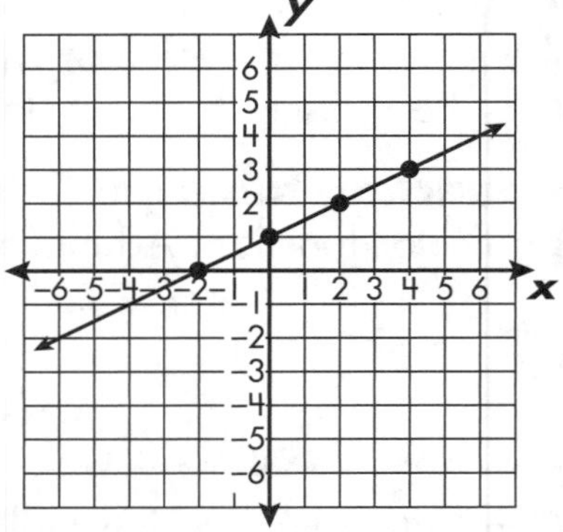

Complete the function table for each function. Then, graph the function.

a

1. $y = x + 3$

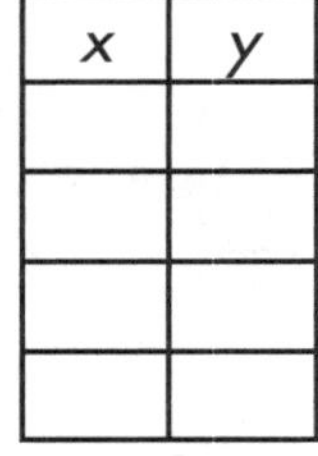

x	y

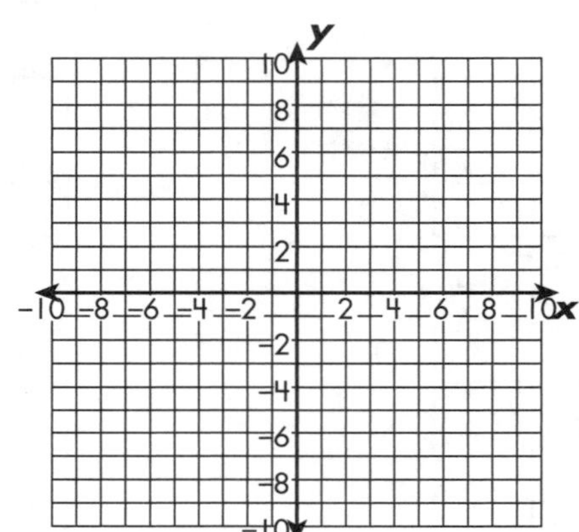

b

$y = 4x - 1$

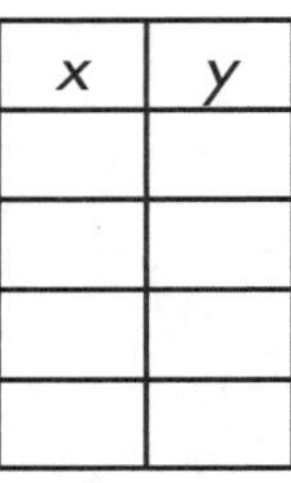

x	y

2. $y = \frac{x}{2} - 1$

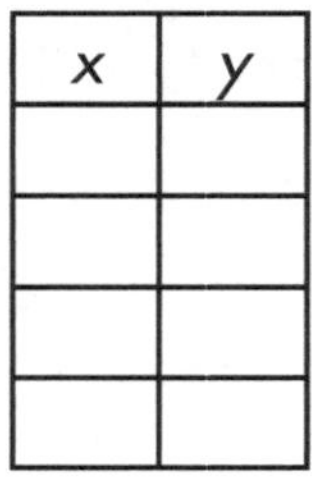

x	y

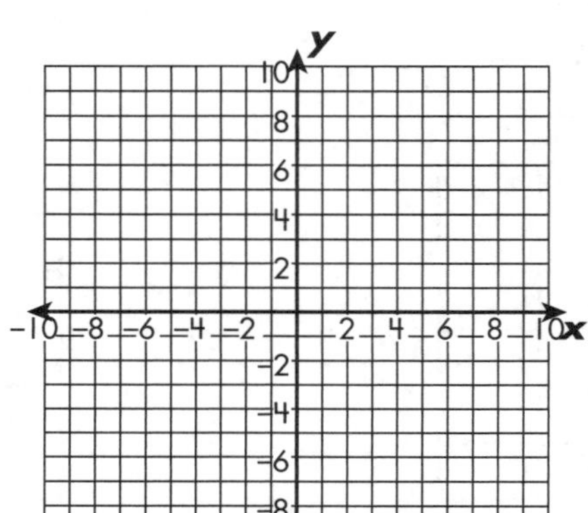

$y = \frac{x}{3} - 1$

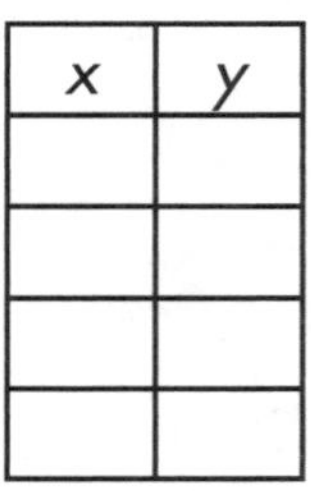

x	y

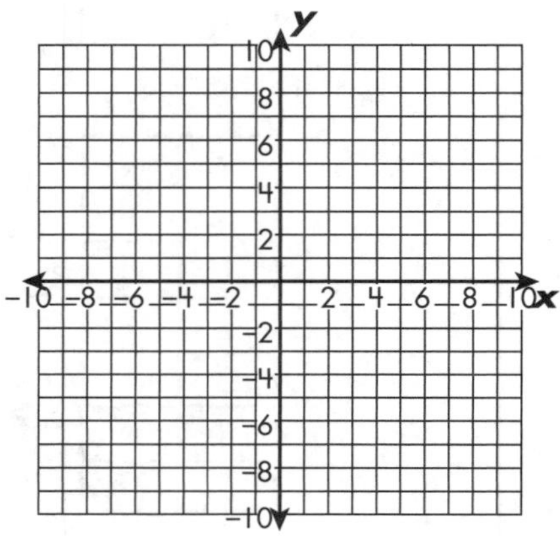

NAME ______________________________

Lesson 8.3 Slope and y-Intercept

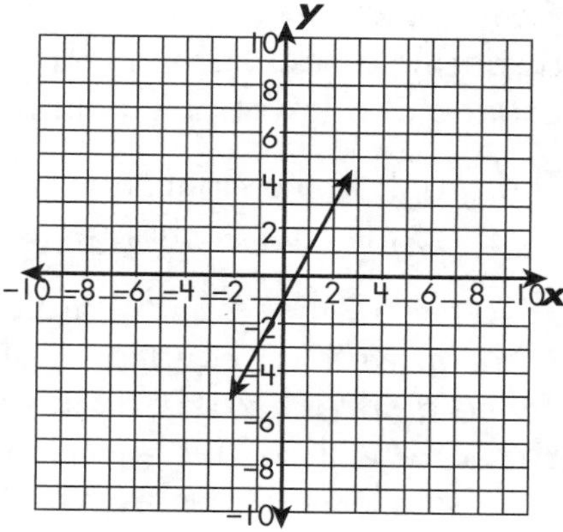

Every straight line can be represented by the equation $y = mx + b$, where m is the slope of the line and b is the y-intercept.

The **slope** of a line is its steepness or slant. It is calculated as follows:

$$m = \frac{\text{change in } y\text{-value}}{\text{change in } x\text{-value}} = \frac{y_2 - y_1}{x_2 - x_1}$$

where (x_1, y_1) and (x_2, y_2) are two different points on the line.

The ***y*-intercept** is the value of y at the point where the line crosses the x-axis (that is, where $x = 0$).

In the graph to the right, the slope (m) for the line $= \frac{(3 - 1)}{(2 - 1)} = 2$.

The line intersects the y-axis at the point (0, −1), so −1 is the y-intercept.

Find the slope and y-intercept for each line.

1.

a

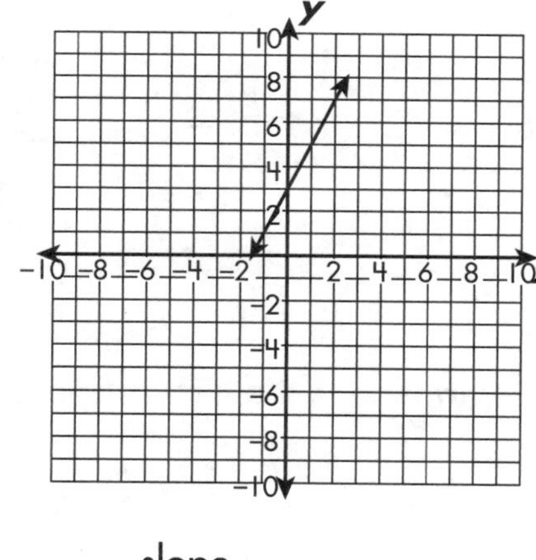

slope ________

y-intercept ________

b

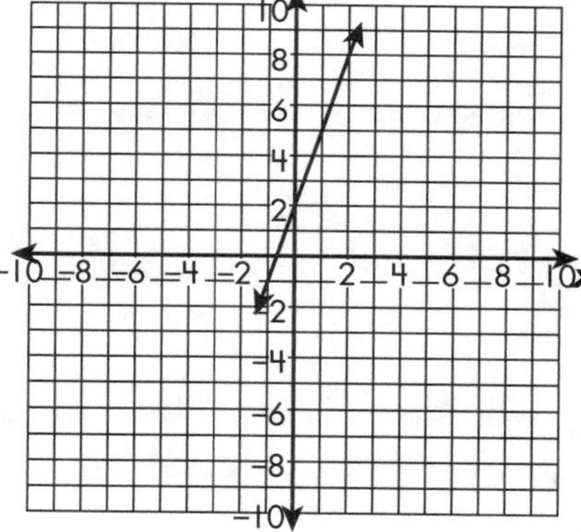

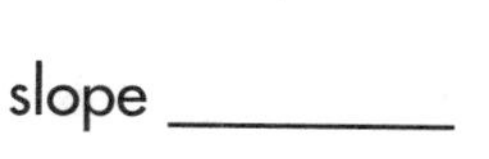

slope ________

y-intercept ________

c

slope ________

y-intercept ________

2. The total cost to produce a shipment of shoes is the fixed cost (the costs that you have even if you produce no shoes, such as equipment) plus the variable cost (the costs that increase as you produce more shoes, such as materials).

a. If you were to graph these costs, which would be the y-intercept? ________

b. Which would be the slope? ________

NAME ____________________

Lesson 8.4 Rate of Change

Rate of change is the speed at which a variable changes over a specific amount of time. The slope of a line shows the rate of change of one variable with respect to another variable.

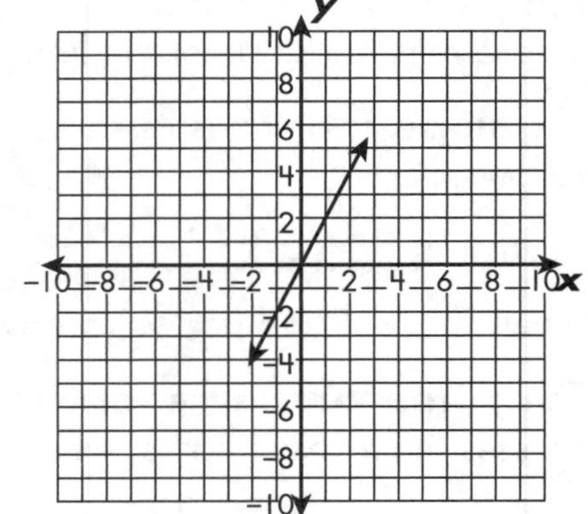

The graph to the right shows that as x increases by 1, y increases by 2, so the rate of change (or slope) is 2.

If you know that y and x are directly proportional to each other, you can write an equation that relates the two quantities. This is called a **direct variation** equation, since y is said to **vary directly** with x. This equation has the form $y = kx$, where $k \neq 0$. k is called the **constant of variation** or the **constant of proportionality**. For the line in the graph, the direct variation equation is $y = 2x$.

Answer each question.

1. If y varies directly with x and you know that $y = 35$ when $x = 5$, what is the constant of variation? ________

2. If you know that the direct variation equation is $y = 3x$ and $y = 12$, what is x? ________

3. Using the same equation, what is y if $x = 5$? ________

4. Distance (d) varies directly with time (t), and the constant of variation is the rate of speed (r). Write a direct variation equation that expresses this. ________

5. A train travels 400 km in 2 hours.

   a. What is the rate? ________

   b. Write a direct variation equation that expresses this relationship, using d for distance and t for time (in hours). ________

   c. Graph the equation.

   d. How many hours would it take the train to travel 300 km? It would take ________ hours.

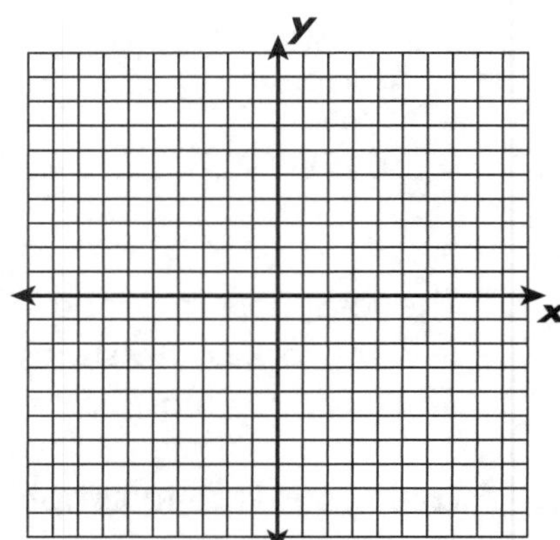

NAME ______________________________

Lesson 8.5 Writing Linear Equations

You can write a linear equation if you know the slope and one point on the line:

1. In the equation $y = mx + b$, replace m with the given slope and x and y with the coordinates of the given point.
2. Solve the equation for the y-intercept (b).
3. Write the equation, replacing m with the slope and b with the y-intercept.

You can also write a linear equation if you know two points on the line:

1. Use the formula $\frac{y_2 - y_1}{x_2 - x_1}$ to calculate m.
2. Choose either of the two points to use in place of x and y in the equation $y = mx + b$. Replace m with the slope you calculated.
3. Solve the equation for the y-intercept (b).
4. Write the equation, replacing m with the slope and b with the y-intercept.

Write a linear equation from the information given below.

1. The slope is 2 and the line passes through point (6, 13). ____________________

2. The slope is 1 and the line passes through point (−4, −6). ____________________

3. The line passes through points (2, 7) and (4, 8). ____________________

4. The line passes through points (0, 5) and (−2, 1). ____________________

5. The function table for the line is given below.

x	y
0	−7
2	−5
5	−2
7	0
10	3
15	8

____

6. The graph for the line is shown below.

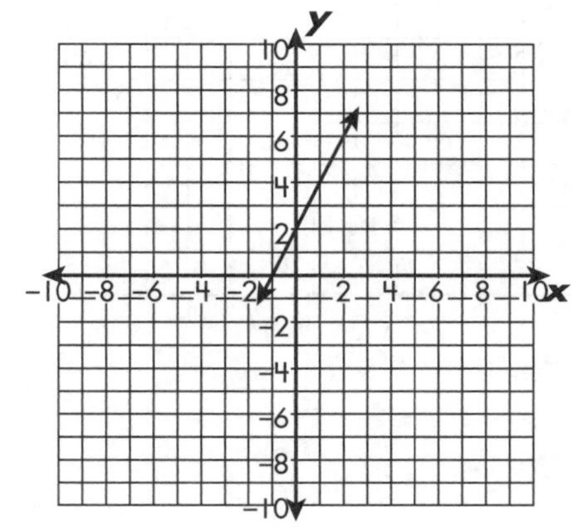

____

NAME ____________________

Lesson 8.6 Best-Fit Lines in Scatterplots

A **scatterplot** is a graph that shows the relationship between two sets of data. If the data points form a straight line or cluster around a line, the relationship between the sets of data is **linear**. If the points cluster around a curve, not a straight line, the relationship is **nonlinear**.

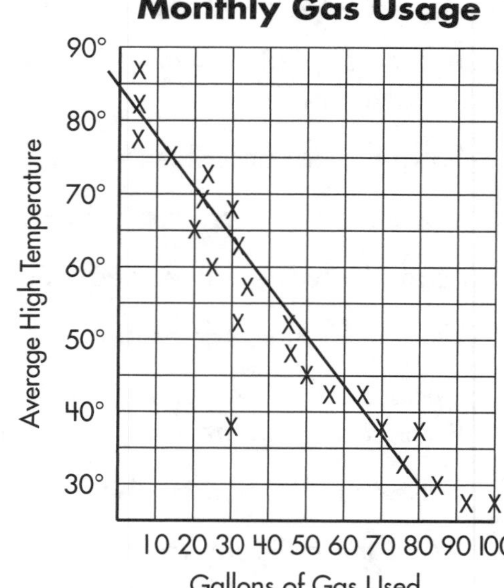

To see a linear relationship more clearly, a **best-fit line** can be drawn. This line is drawn so that there are about the same number of data points above and below the line. When the best-fit line slopes upward from left to right, the correlation between the sets of data is **positive**, or direct. This means that as one set of data increases, the other set of data also increases. When the best-fit line slopes downward from left to right, the correlation is **negative**, or inverse. This means that as one set of data increases, the other set of data decreases.

The scatterplot here shows the relationship between average high temperature and a family's gas use for heating fuel each month. The points cluster around a straight line, so the relationship is linear. As temperature increases, gas use decreases, so the correlation is negative.

Study the scatterplots below. Then, answer the questions.

1. Is the relationship in the scatterplot linear or nonlinear?

a

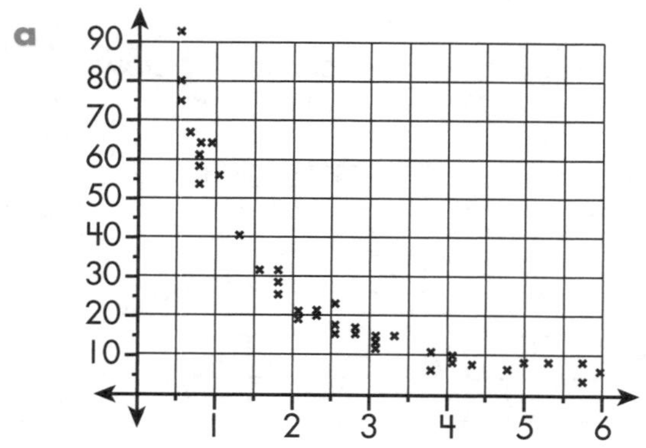

b

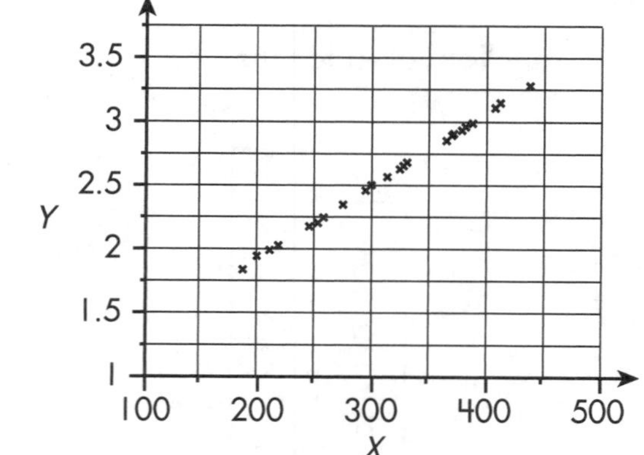

____________________ ____________________

NAME ____________________

Lesson 8.6 Best-Fit Lines in Scatterplots

Create a scatterplot from the following data. Then, answer the questions that follow.

2. Is the correlation in the scatterplot positive or negative?

a

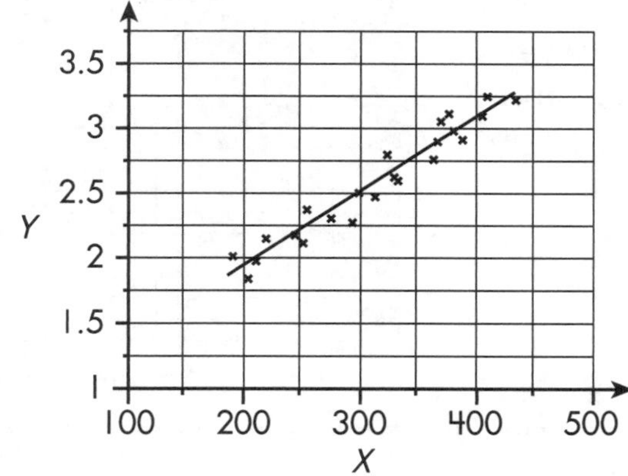

____

b

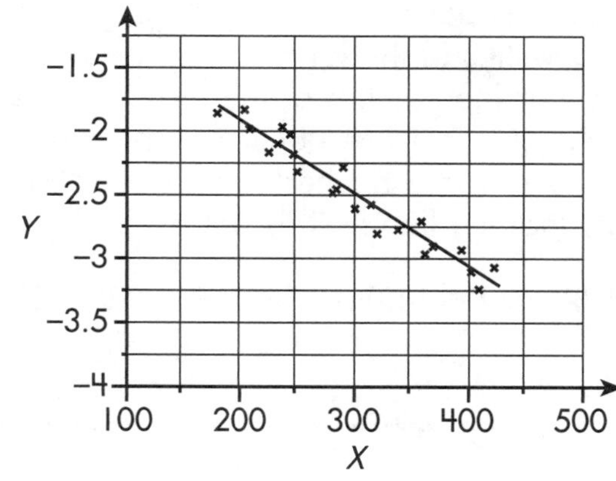

____

3. (10, 450); (12, 650); (14, 750); (16, 1,050); (18, 1,250); (20, 1,500)

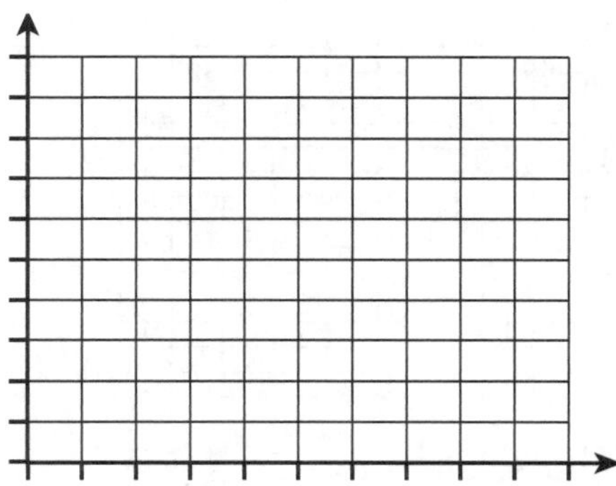

4. Is the relationship shown in the graph linear or nonlinear? ________

5. Is the correlation positive or negative? ________

6. Suppose you learn that the two sets of data being compared by this scatterplot are number of years of education and weekly earnings.

   a. How many people were polled? ________

   b. How would you describe the relationship between the number of years of education these people have and their weekly earnings?

____

NAME ______________________

Lesson 8.7 Graphing Linear Inequalities

A linear inequality is an inequality that has the form $y \geq mx + b$, $y \leq mx + b$, $y > mx + b$, or $y < mx + b$.

To graph a linear inequality, first graph the line for $y = mx + b$. For inequalities of the form $y \geq mx + b$, shade the area above the line. For inequalities of the form $y \leq mx + b$, shade the area below the line. For inequalities of the form $y > mx + b$ or $y < mx + b$, use a dashed line, rather than a solid line, to indicate that the line itself is not part of the inequality.

The graph to the right shows the inequality $y \geq 2x + 3$.

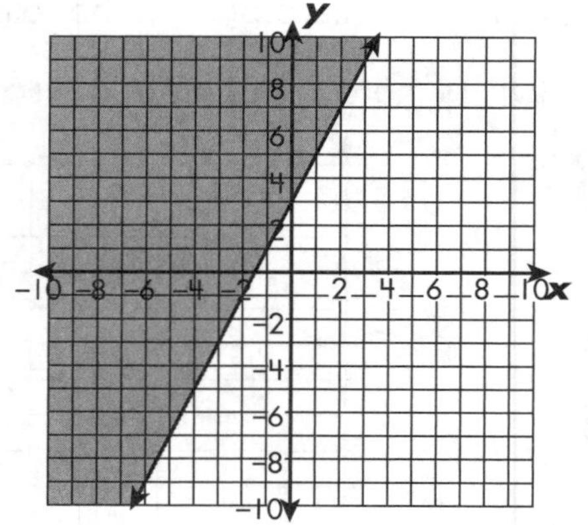

1. Graph the solution to $y < x - 3$.

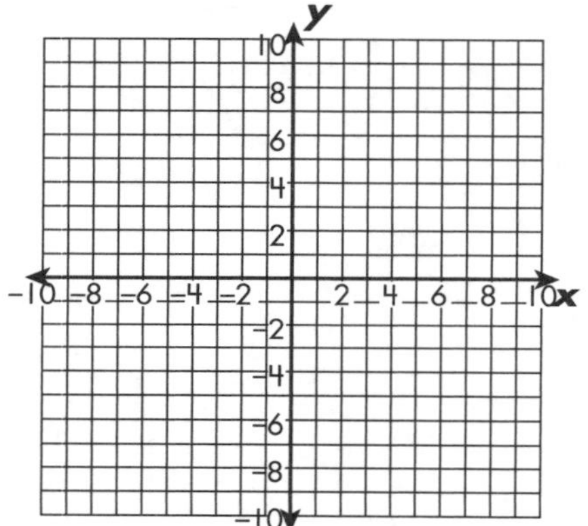

2. Graph the solution to $y > \frac{x}{2} + 2$

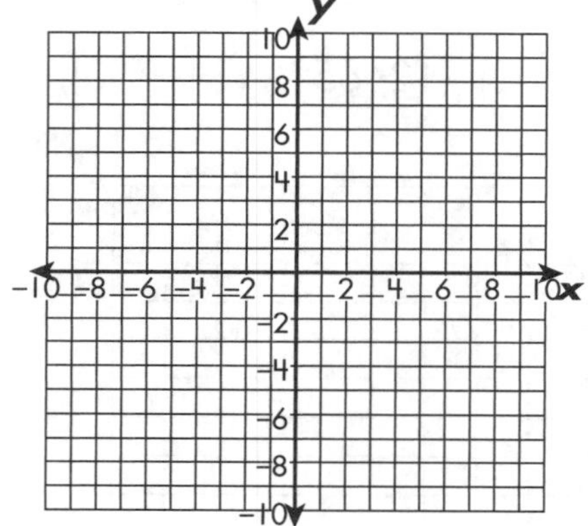

3. Graph the solution to $y \leq 2x + 1$.

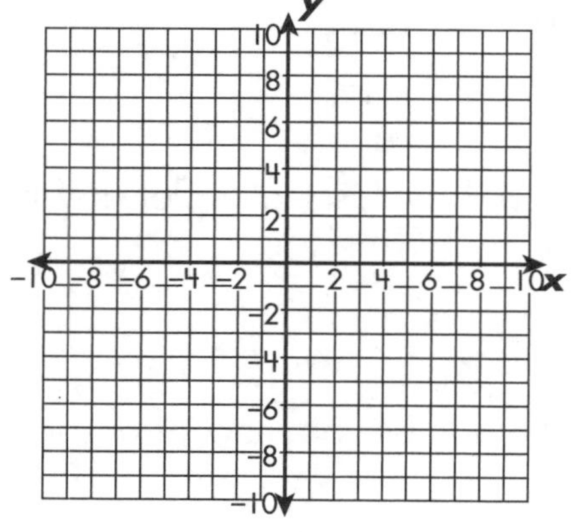

4. Graph the solution to $y \geq \frac{x}{2} - 2$.

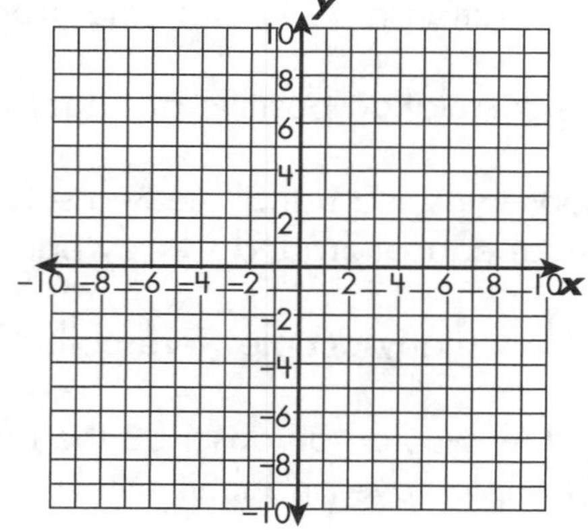

NAME ______________________________

Check What You Learned

Functions and Graphing

Complete the function table for each function. Then, graph the function.

a

1. $y = x + 4$

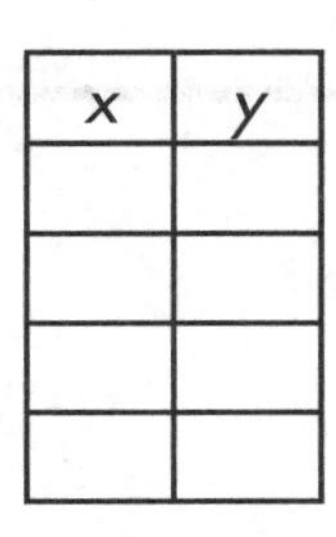

x	y

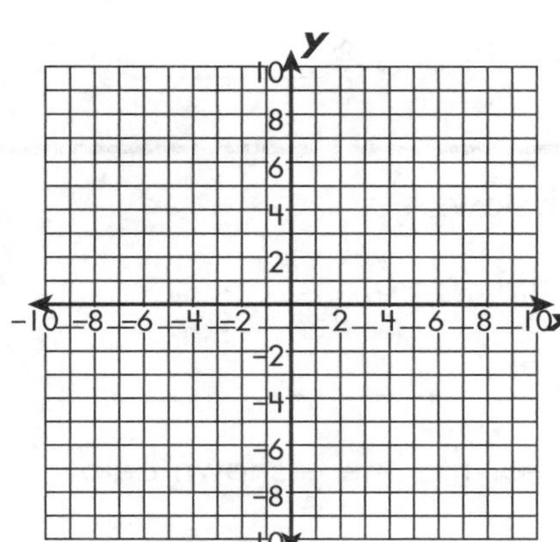

b

$y = 4x - 2$

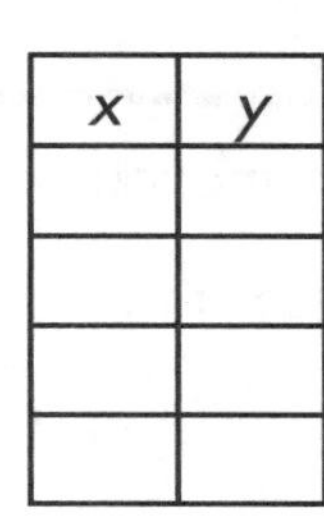

x	y

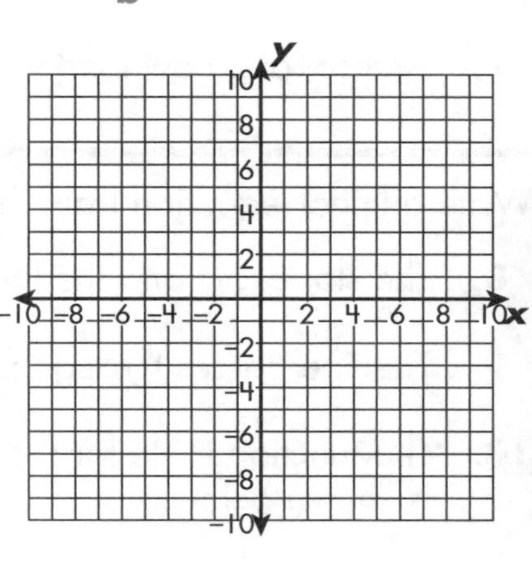

Graph the solution to each inequality.

a

2. $y < x + 2$

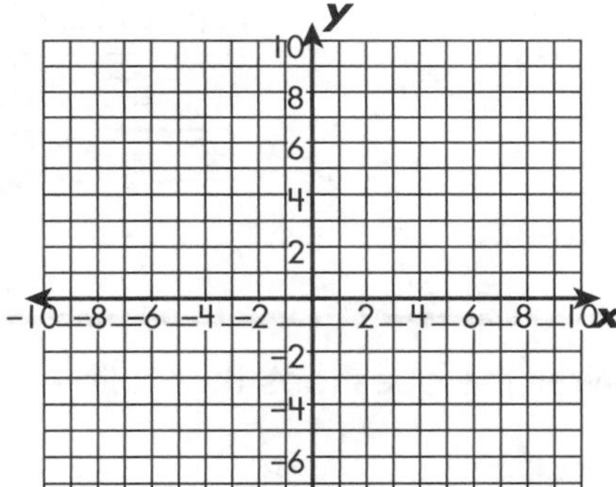

b

$y \geq 2x - 2$

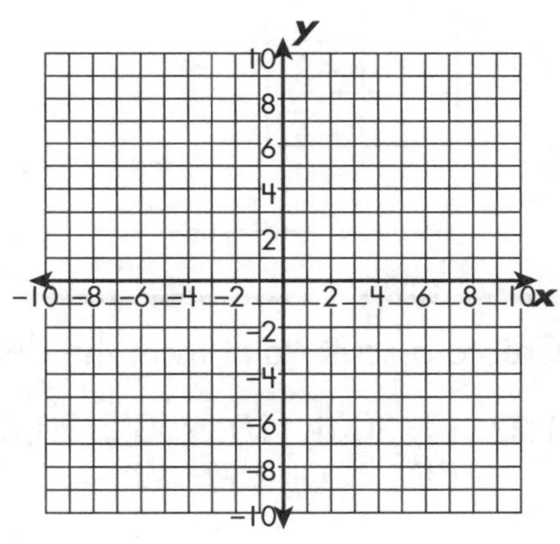

Answer each question.

3. If y varies directly with x and you know that $y = 48$ when $x = 6$, what is the constant of variation? ________

4. If you know that the direct variation equation is $y = 4x$ and $y = 28$, what is x? ________

5. Using the same equation, what is y if $x = 6$? ________

Check What You Learned

Functions and Graphing

6. Evan biked 8 miles in 30 minutes. Express his rate of speed as a direct variation equation, using d for distance and t for time (in hours). ________

7. At that rate, how long would it take him to bike 24 miles? ________

Write a linear equation from the information given below.

8. The slope is 4 and the line passes through point (–2, –6). ________

9. The line passes through points (0, 4) and (–2, 2). ________

10. The function table for the line is shown below.

x	y
–2	–7
–1	–6
0	–5
1	–4
2	–3
3	–2

____

11. The graph for the line is shown below.

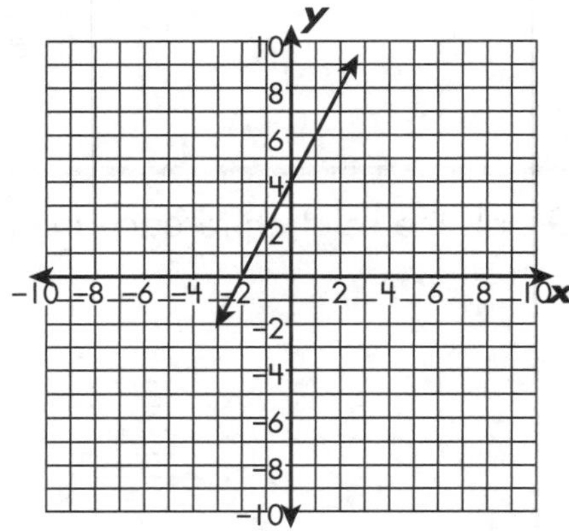

____

Create a scatterplot from the data below. Then, answer the questions that follow.

12. (0, 300), (10, 250), (20, 200), (30, 150), (40, 100), (50, 50)

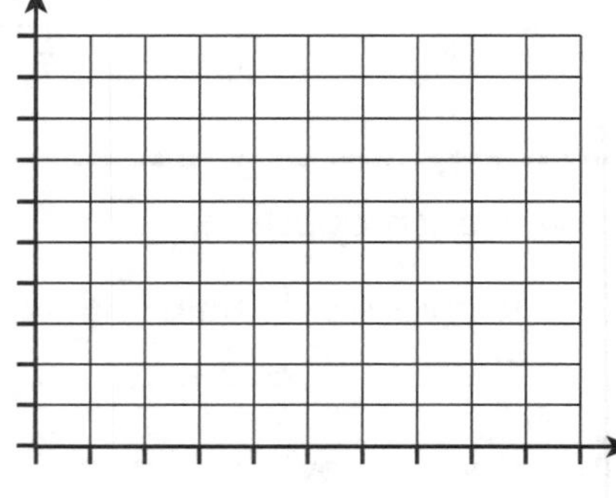

13. Is the relationship linear or nonlinear? ________

14. Is the correlation positive or negative? ________

15. Suppose you learn that the data sets being compared are the number of items sold (x) and the price per item (y). Describe the relationship between the two sets of data by completing the sentence below.

    As the price per item ________, the number of items sold ________.

NAME ________________

Check What You Know

Algebra and Geometry

Answer each question using letters to name lines and numbers to name angles.

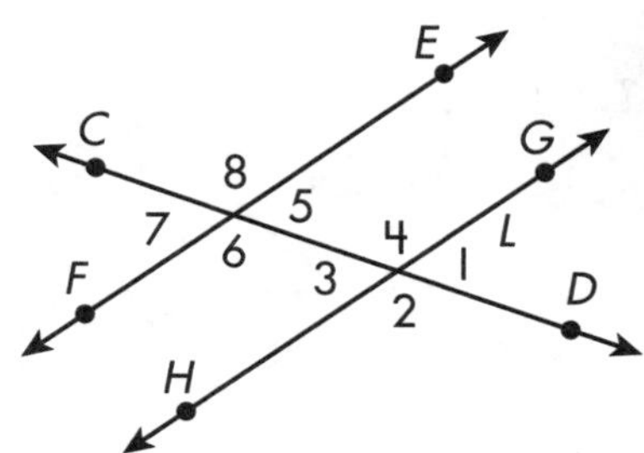

1. Identify the parallel lines. ________
2. Identify the transversal. ________
3. Identify 2 pairs of alternate interior angles. ________
4. Identify 2 pairs of alternate exterior angles. ________

Use the Pythagorean Theorem to find the length of the missing side of each right triangle.

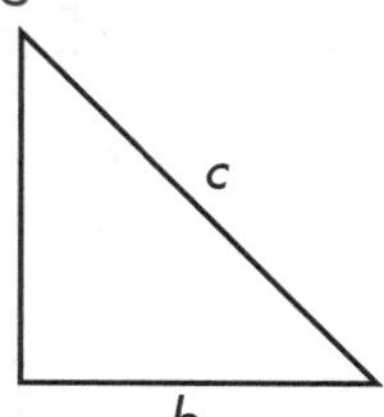

5. If $a = 8$ and $b = 6$, $c = \sqrt{}$ ________, or ________.
6. If $b = 10$ and $c = 15$, $a = \sqrt{}$ ________, or about ________.
7. If $a = 14$ and $c = 24$, $b = \sqrt{}$ ________, or about ________.

Label each triangle acute, right, or obtuse and equilateral, isosceles, or scalene.

	a	b	c
8.	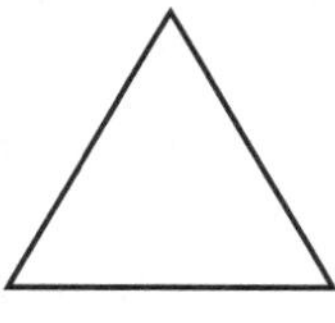		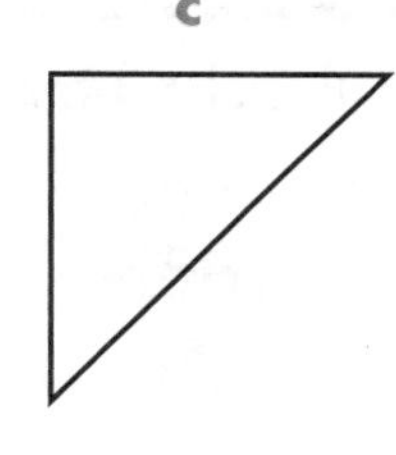
	________, ________	________, ________	________, ________

Use ratios to determine whether the pairs of triangles are similar.

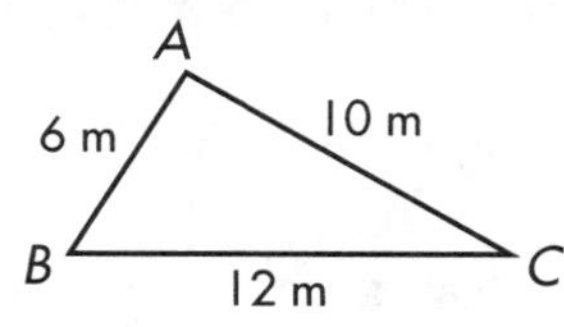

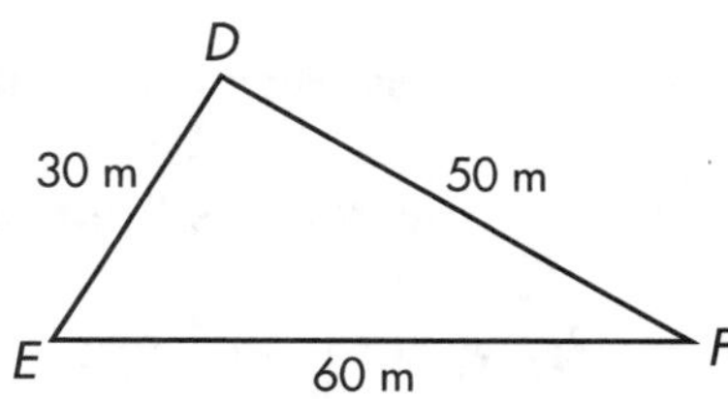

9. $\frac{AB}{DE}$ = ________ $\frac{BC}{EF}$ = ________ $\frac{AC}{DF}$ = ________

Are the triangles similar? ________

NAME ______________________

Check What You Know

Algebra and Geometry

Find the perimeter of each figure.

10.

a

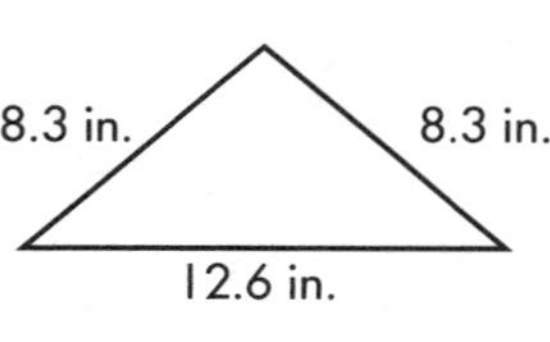

________ in.

b

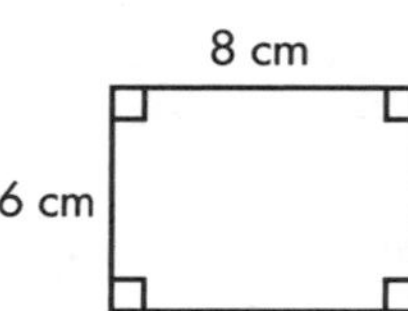

________ cm

c

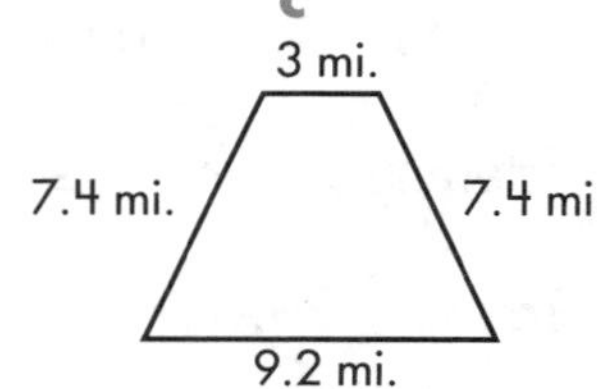

________ mi.

Find the unknown measure.

11.

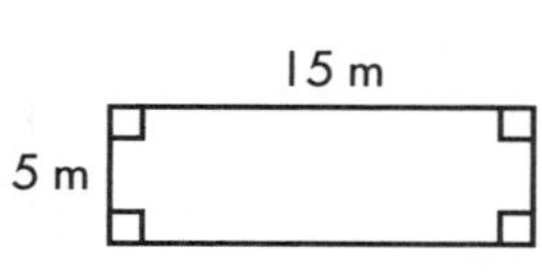

area = ________ m^2

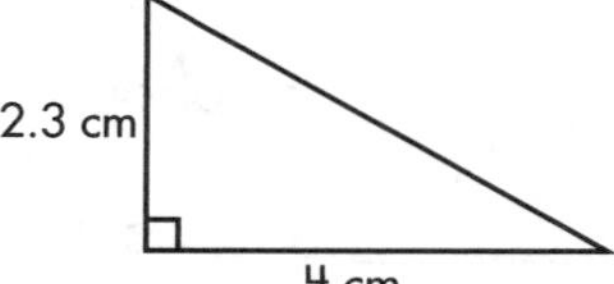

area = ________ cm^2

9 ft. Area = 108 $ft.^2$

length = ________ ft.

Complete the chart for each circle. Use 3.14 for π. Round to the nearest hundredth.

	a **Radius**	b **Diameter**	c **Circumference**	d **Area**
12.	8 m	________ m	________ m	________ m^2
13.	________ yd.	12 yd.	________ yd.	________ $yd.^2$

14. Jorge wants to make a square dog pen that measures 12 feet on one side.

a. How much fencing must Jorge buy to make the pen? ________ feet

b. How much space will Jorge's dog have in his pen? ________ square feet

15. A circular pool measures 4.2 meters across. Along the edge is a painted line.

a. How long is the painted line? ________ meters

b. What is the area of the pool's surface? ________ square meters

NAME ________________

Lesson 9.1 Squares and Square Roots

The **square** of a number is that number times itself. A square is expressed as, for example, 6^2, which means 6×6, or 6 squared. The **square root** of a number is the value that, multiplied by itself, equals that number. The square root of 36 is 6. This is expressed as $\sqrt{36} = 6$.

Not all square roots of numbers are whole numbers, like 6. Numbers that have a whole number as their square root are called **perfect squares**.

The square root of any number that is not a perfect square is called a **radical number**. The symbol $\sqrt{}$ is called a **radical sign**. When a number is not a perfect square, you can estimate its square root by determining which perfect squares it comes between. $\sqrt{50}$ is a little more than 7, because $\sqrt{49}$ is exactly 7. $\sqrt{60}$ is between 7 and 8 but is closer to 8, because 60 is closer to 64 than to 49.

A table of squares and square roots appears at the back of this book. Use the table to identify the square root of these perfect squares.

	a	b	c
1.	$\sqrt{9}$ = ________	$\sqrt{81}$ = ________	$\sqrt{36}$ = ________
2.	$\sqrt{25}$ = ________	$\sqrt{4}$ = ________	$\sqrt{64}$ = ________
3.	$\sqrt{1}$ = ________	$\sqrt{16}$ = ________	$\sqrt{100}$ = ________

Estimate the following square roots without looking at the table at the back of the book.

4. $\sqrt{80}$ is between ________ and ________ but closer to ________.

5. $\sqrt{27}$ is between ________ and ________ but closer to ________.

6. $\sqrt{53}$ is between ________ and ________ but closer to ________.

7. $\sqrt{96}$ is between ________ and ________ but closer to ________.

8. $\sqrt{41}$ is between ________ and ________ but closer to ________.

NAME ____________________

Lesson 9.2 Points, Lines, Rays, and Angles

A **point** is a single location in space. It has no dimensions. A **line** is the set of all points extending straight in both directions. A **line segment** is the part of a line between 2 points on the line.

You can name a point with a letter: point B.

You can name a line by naming any 2 points on the line: $\overleftrightarrow{BC}$ or $\overleftrightarrow{CB}$.

You can name a line segment by naming its end points: $\overline{BC}$ or $\overline{CB}$.

A **ray** is part of a line. It has one endpoint but extends infinitely in one direction. An **angle** is the union of two rays that share a common endpoint. The endpoint is called a **vertex**.

You can name a ray by naming its endpoint first and another point on the ray: $\overrightarrow{ST}$. This ray is not $\overrightarrow{TS}$.

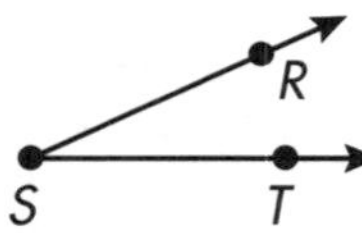

You can name an angle by naming a point on one ray, followed by the shared endpoint and a point on the other ray: $\angle RST$ or $\angle TSR$. Also, you can use the vertex alone to name the angle: $\angle S$.

Tell what each expression means.

	a	b	c
1.	$\angle XYZ$ ________	$\overleftrightarrow{EF}$ ________	$\angle D$ ________
2.	C ________	$\overrightarrow{AB}$ ________	$\overline{MN}$ ________

Name each figure using letters. Name each figure in more than one way, if you can.

3.

____

Q R

____

____

4.

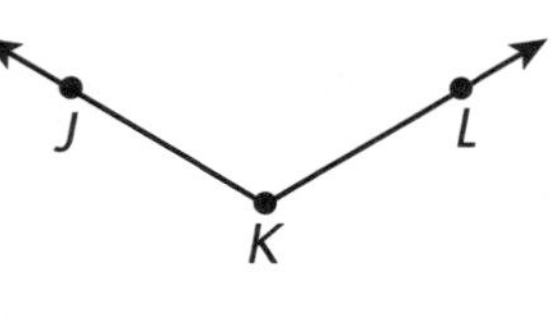

____

P

____

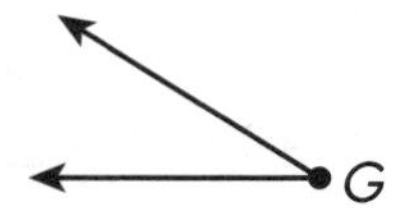

____

NAME ___________________________

Lesson 9.3 Vertical, Supplementary, and Complementary Angles

An **acute angle** measures less than 90°.

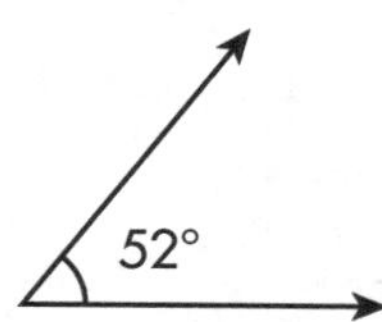

A **right angle** measures exactly 90°.

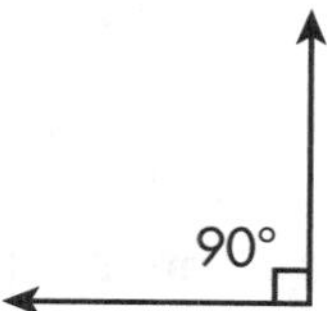

An **obtuse angle** measures more than 90° and less than 180°.

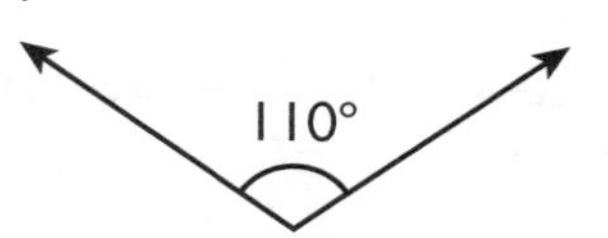

Vertical angles are the 2 angles opposite each other where 2 lines meet. $\angle A$ and $\angle C$ are vertical angles. $\angle B$ and $\angle D$ are also vertical angles. Vertical angles are congruent; they have the same measure. Supplementary angles are 2 angles whose measures add up to 180°. $\angle A$ and $\angle B$ are supplementary. $\angle B$ and $\angle C$ are also supplementary.

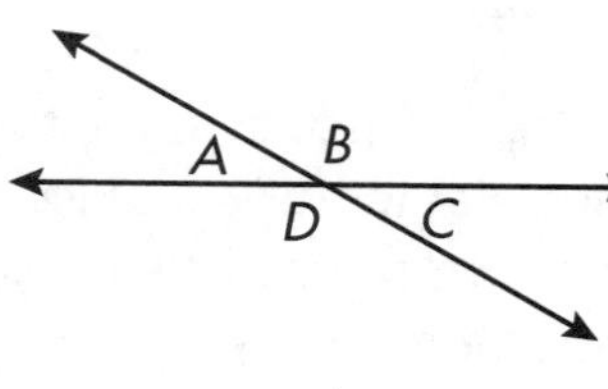

Complementary angles are 2 angles whose measures add up to 90°. $\angle E$ and $\angle F$ are complementary. An angle bisector is a ray that divides an angle exactly in half. In this example, IH is an angle bisector of $\angle GIJ$.

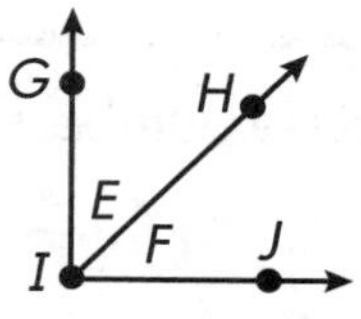

Measure each angle with a protractor. Write the measure. Then, identify the angle as acute, right, or obtuse.

	a	b	c
1.	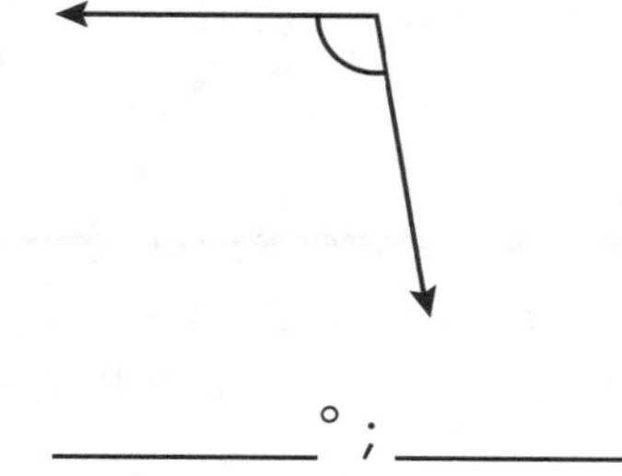	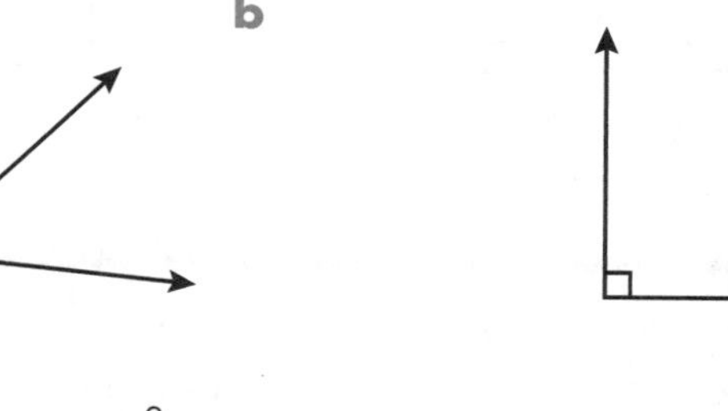	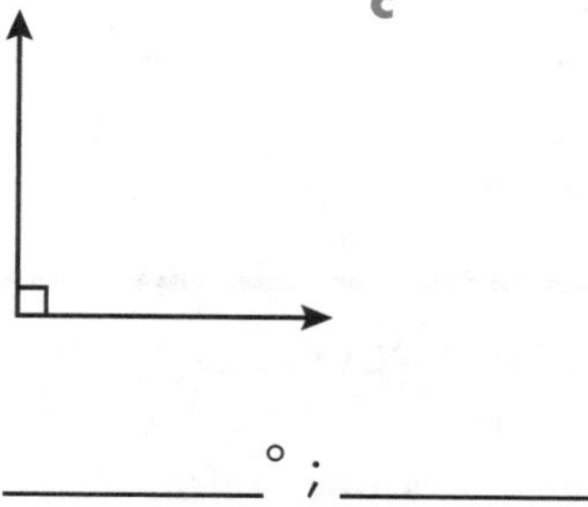
	________° ; ________	________° ; ________	________° ; ________

Use 3 letters to name angles in the figure at right.

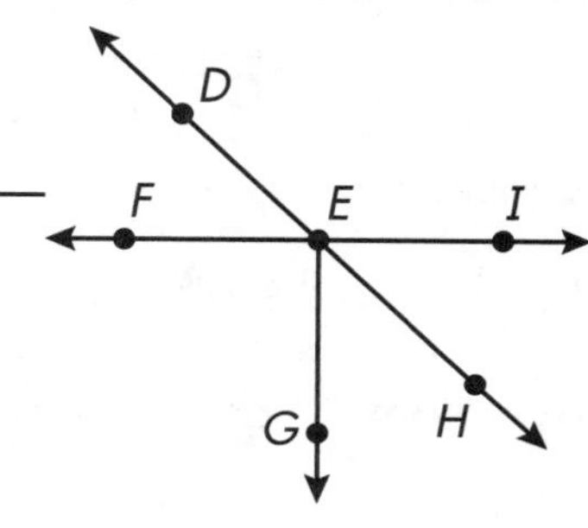

2. Name the right angles. $\angle$________ and $\angle$ ________

3. Name the pair of complementary angles. $\angle$________/$\angle$________

4. Name the angle bisector. ________

5. Name 1 pair of vertical angles. $\angle$________/$\angle$________

6. Name 1 pair of supplementary angles. $\angle$________/$\angle$________

NAME ______________________

Lesson 9.4 Transversals

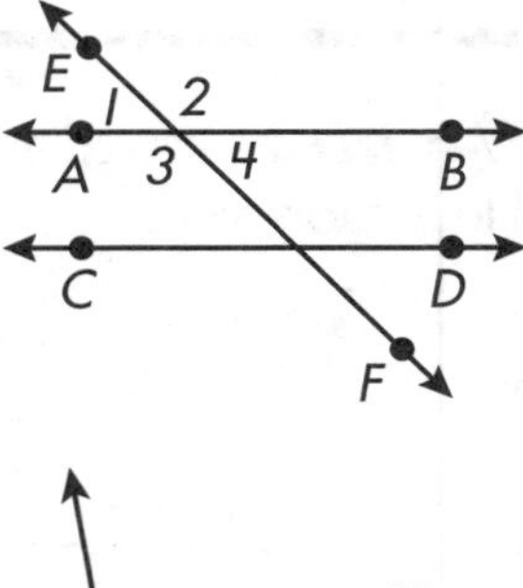

Parallel lines are 2 lines that will never meet. In this figure, $\overleftrightarrow{AB}$ and $\overleftrightarrow{CD}$ are parallel lines.

A **transversal** is a line that crosses at least 2 other lines. $\overleftrightarrow{EF}$ is a transversal of $\overleftrightarrow{AB}$ and $\overleftrightarrow{CD}$.

Adjacent angles are any 2 angles that are next to one another. In the top figure, ∠1 and ∠2 are adjacent. ∠2 and ∠4 are also adjacent. In the bottom figure, ∠X and ∠Y are adjacent. Adjacent angles share a ray and a vertex.

When a transversal cuts across parallel lines, the adjacent angles are supplementary. ∠1 and ∠2 are supplementary; they sum to 180°. The bottom figure has no parallel lines. ∠X and ∠Y are adjacent but not supplementary.

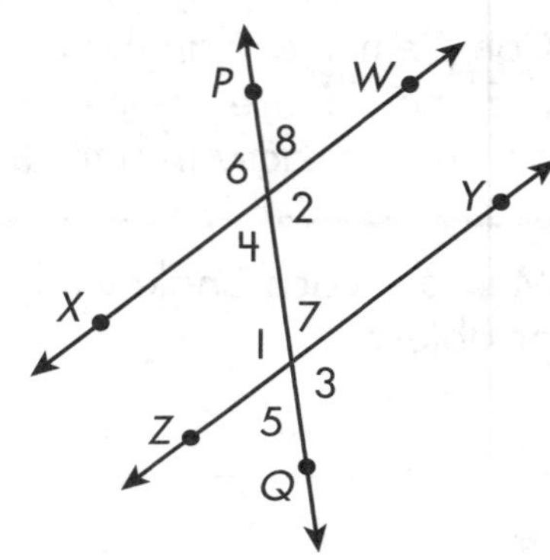

Use numbers to name angles in the figure. Use letters to name lines.

1. Name the parallel lines: ________ and ________

2. Name the transversal: ________

3. Name 3 pairs of adjacent angles:

   ∠________/∠________ ; ∠________/∠________ ;

   ∠________/∠________

Alternate interior angles are angles that are inside the parallel lines and on opposite sides of the transversal. ∠4 and ∠7 are alternate interior angles. Alternate interior angles are congruent; they have the same measure.

4. Name the other pair of alternate interior angles in the figure. ∠________/∠________

Alternate exterior angles are angles that are outside the parallel lines and on opposite sides of the transversal. ∠6 and ∠3 are alternate exterior angles. Alternate exterior angles are also congruent.

5. Name the other pair of alternate exterior angles in the figure. ∠________/∠________

6. Name 2 pairs of vertical angles in the figure.

   ∠________/∠________; ∠________/∠________

NAME ______________________

Lesson 9.5 Triangles

Triangles can be classified by their angles. The angles in a triangle always add up to 180°.

A **right triangle** contains 1 right angle: an angle of exactly 90°.

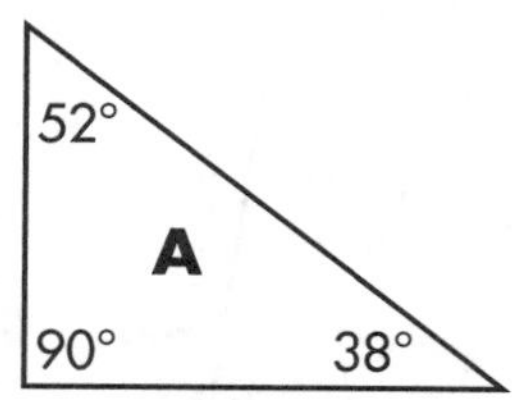

An **acute triangle** contains only acute angles—that is, angles less than 90°.

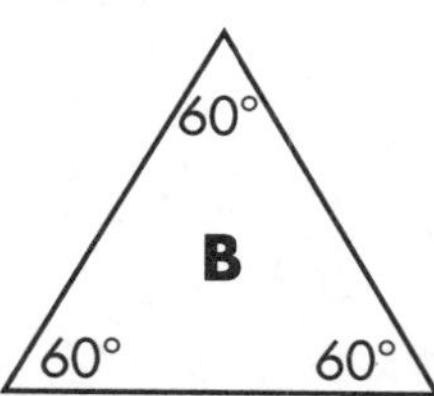

An **obtuse triangle** contains 1 obtuse angle: an angle greater than 90°.

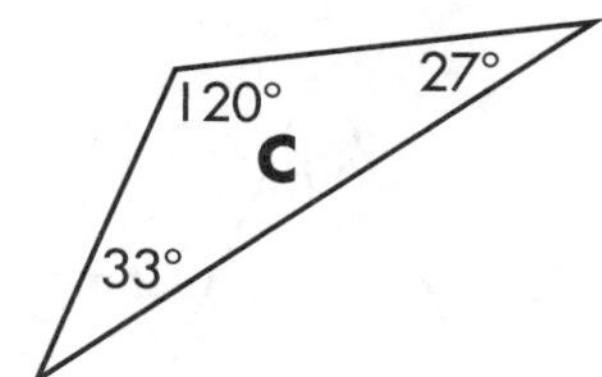

Triangles can also be classified by their sides.

An **equilateral triangle** has 3 sides of the same length.

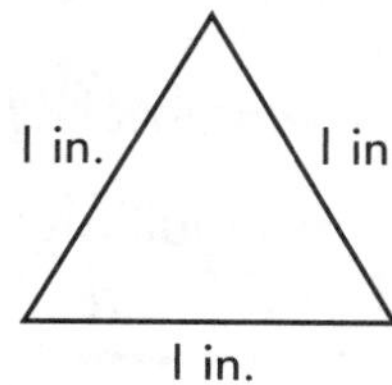

An **isosceles triangle** has 2 sides of the same length.

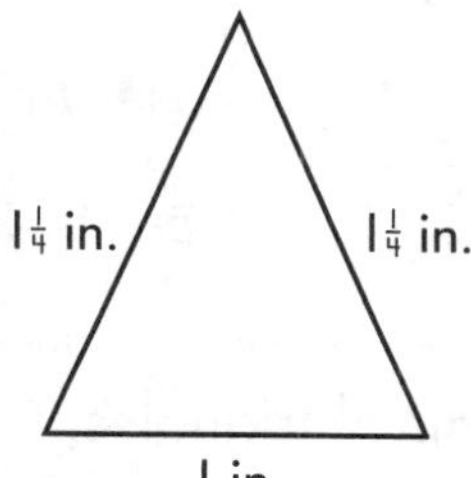

A **scalene triangle** has no sides of the same length.

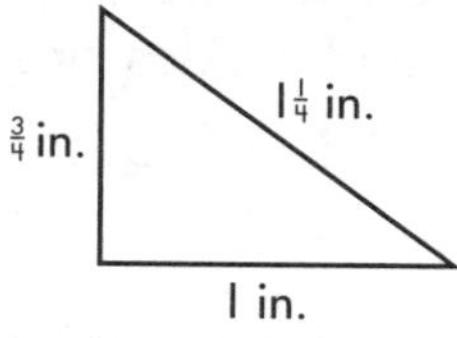

Classify each triangle by its angles and its sides. Use a protractor and ruler if needed.

1.

a

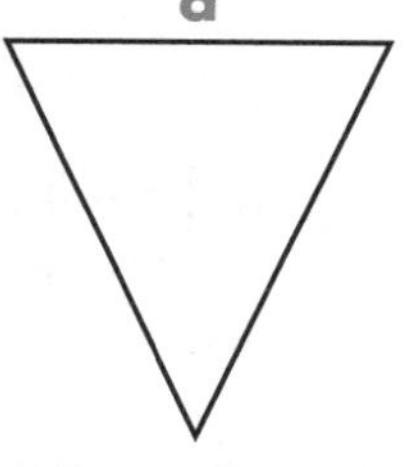

angles: __________

sides: __________

b

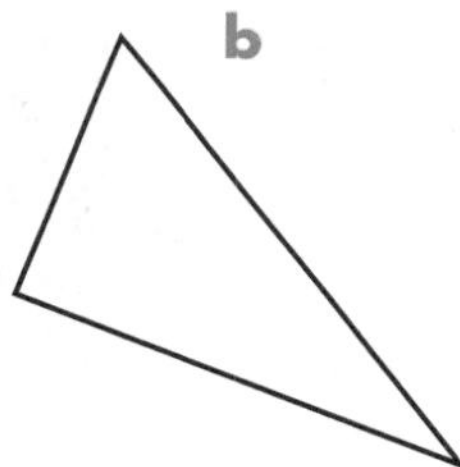

angles: __________

sides: __________

c

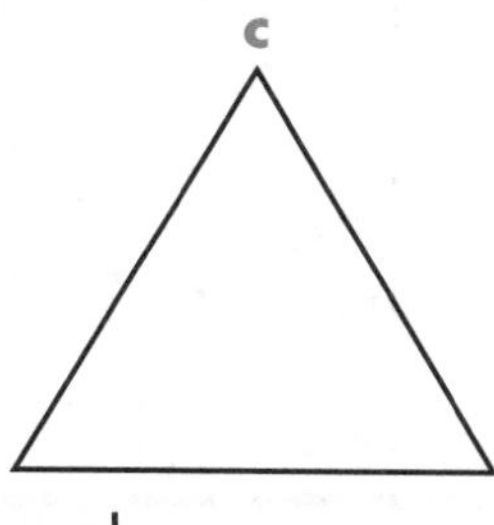

angles: __________

sides: __________

2.

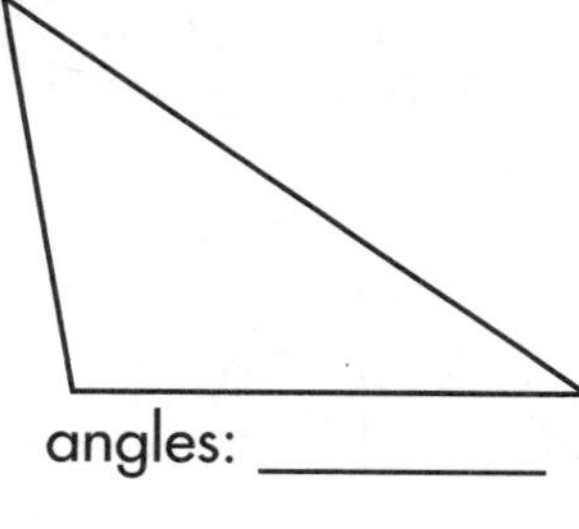

angles: __________

sides: __________

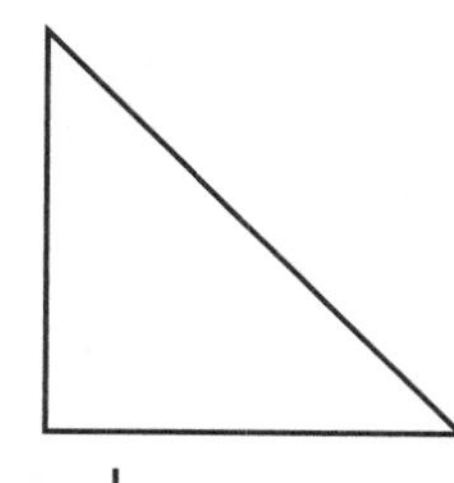

angles: __________

sides: __________

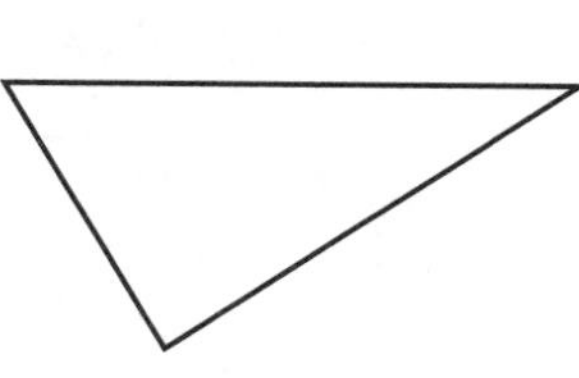

angles: __________

sides: __________

NAME ____________________

Lesson 9.6 Similar Triangles

Two triangles are **similar** if their angles are congruent (equal) and the lengths of their corresponding (matching) sides are proportional (have the same ratio).

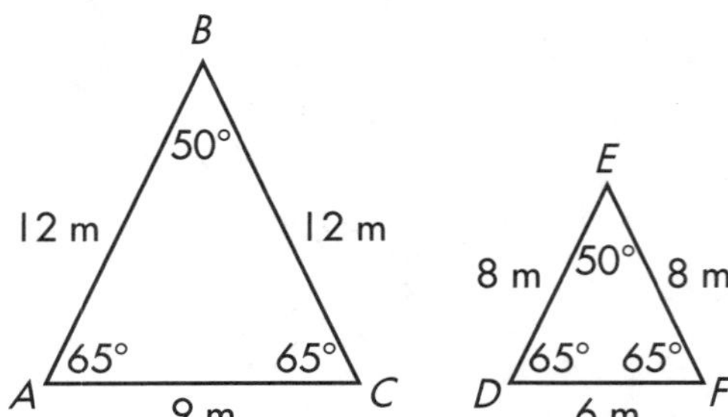

These triangles are similar. The angles are congruent. All sides are proportional.

$\frac{AB}{DE} = \frac{12}{8} = \frac{3}{2}$ $\frac{BC}{EF} = \frac{12}{8} = \frac{3}{2}$ $\frac{AC}{DF} = \frac{9}{6} = \frac{3}{2}$

When you know that triangles are similar, you can use the ratio of the known lengths of the sides to figure the unknown lengths.

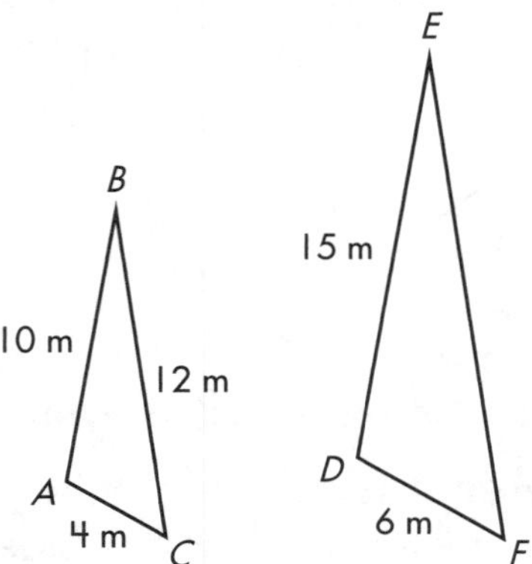

Use a proportion to find the length of *EF*.

$\frac{AC}{DF} = \frac{BC}{EF}$ $\frac{4}{6} = \frac{12}{n}$ Cross multiply:
$4n = 72$ $n = 18$

Find the proportions of the sides of this pair of triangles. Circle *similar* or *not similar*.

1.

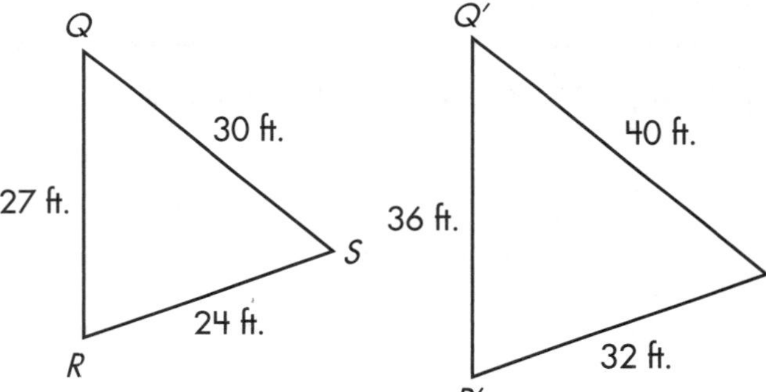

$\frac{QR}{Q'R'}$ = __________ = __________

$\frac{QS}{Q'S'}$ = __________ = __________

$\frac{SR}{S'R'}$ = __________ = __________

similar not similar

For each pair of similar triangles, find the length of the missing side and label it.

	a	b
2.	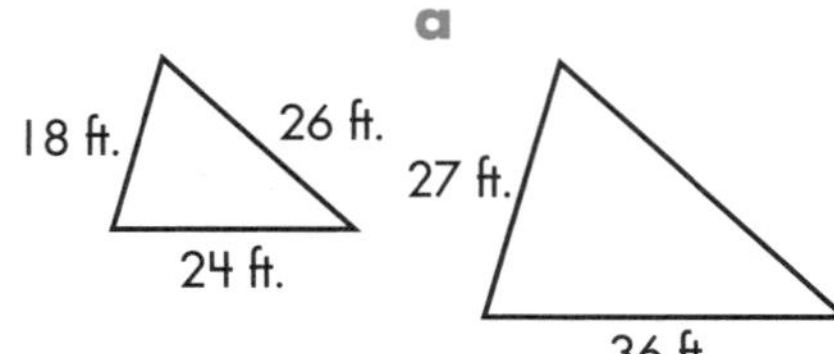	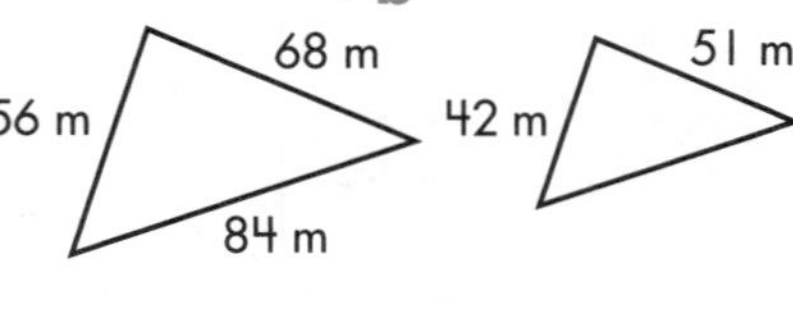
3.	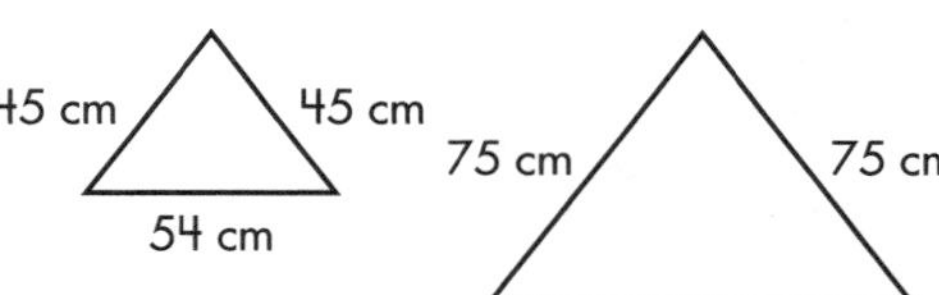	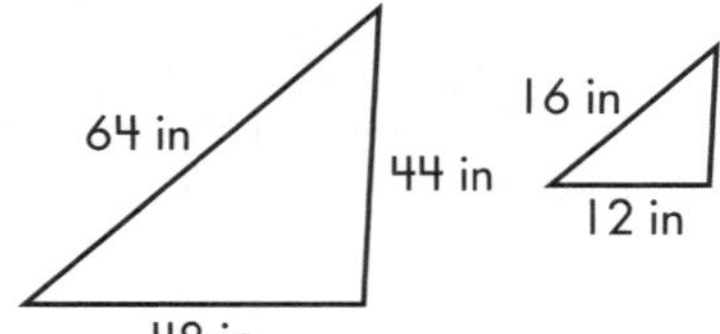

NAME ___________________________

Lesson 9.7 The Pythagorean Theorem

For all right triangles, the **Pythagorean Theorem** states that the square of the hypotenuse equals the sum of the squares of the other 2 sides.

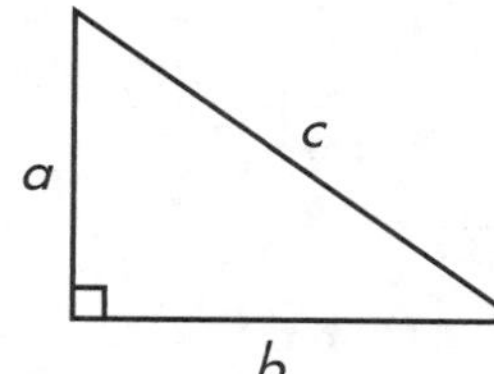

In a right triangle, the hypotenuse is the side opposite the right angle. The other 2 sides are the legs. In this figure, c is the hypotenuse and a and b are the legs. If you know the lengths of 2 sides, you can use the Pythagorean Theorem to find the length of the third side.

If $a = 12$ m and $c = 13$ m, what is b? $a^2 + b^2 = c^2$

$12^2 + b^2 = 13^2$ $144 + b^2 = 169$ $144 + b^2 - 144 = 169 - 144$

$b^2 = 25$ $b = \sqrt{25}$ $b = 5$ m

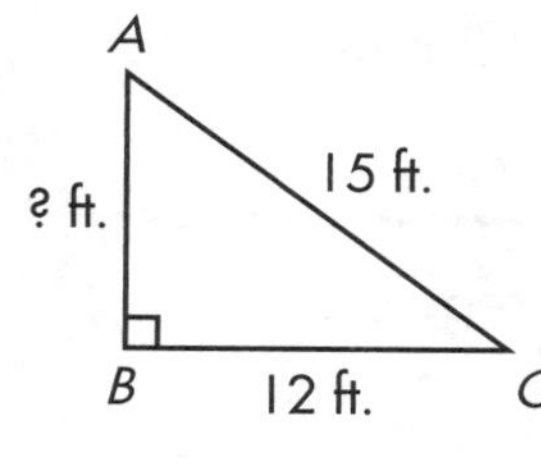

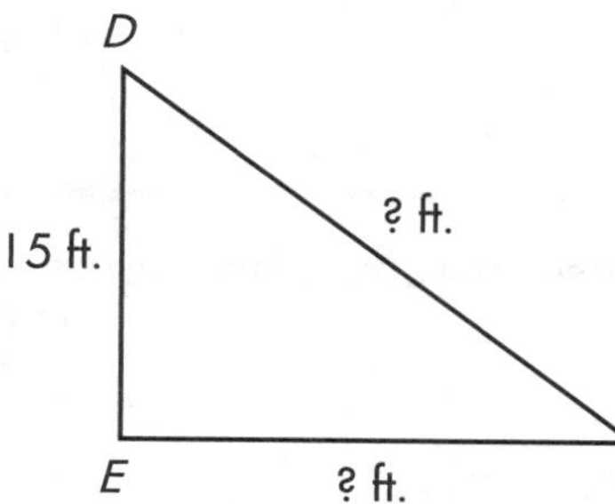

For similar right triangles, you can use the Pythagorean Theorem and ratios to find the unknown sides. First, find the length of $\overline{AB}$.

$a^2 + b^2 = c^2$ $a^2 + 12^2 = 15^2$

$a^2 + 144 = 225$

$a^2 + 144 - 144 = 225 - 144$ $a^2 = 81$ $a = 9$ ft.

Now use ratios to find the unknown lengths of $\overline{EF}$ and $\overline{DF}$.

$\frac{AB}{DE} = \frac{BC}{EF}$ $\frac{9}{15} = \frac{12}{n}$ $9n = 180$ $n = 20.$

$EF = 20$ ft.

$\frac{AB}{DE} = \frac{AC}{DF}$ $\frac{9}{15} = \frac{15}{n}$ $9n = 225$ $n = 25$

$DF = 25$ ft.

Assume that each problem describes a right triangle. Find the unknown lengths. Round to tenths. Refer to the table of squares and square roots at the back of the book, if needed.

	a	b
1.	$a = 10, b = 14, c = \sqrt{}$ ________ or ________	$a = 22, c = 34, b = \sqrt{}$ ________ or ________

2. Find the missing sides in this pair of similar right triangles.

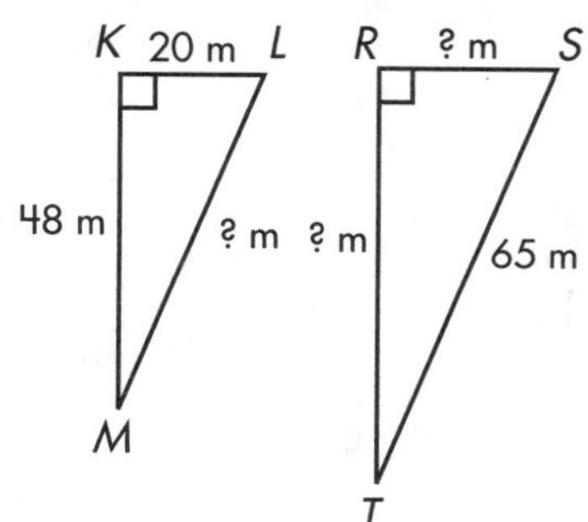

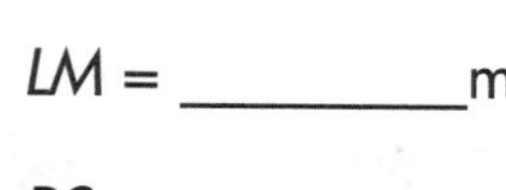

$LM =$ ____________ m

$RS =$ ____________ m

$RT =$ ____________ m

3. About how long is the lake shown below? The lake is about ________ km long.

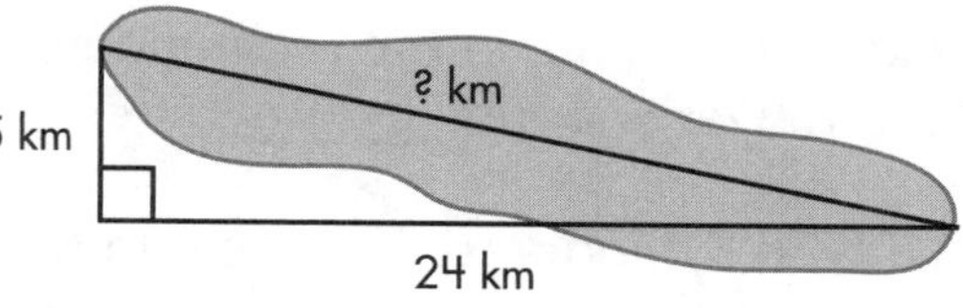

NAME ______________________________

Lesson 9.8 Perimeter

The **perimeter** of a figure is the distance around it.

When you know the lengths of all sides, just add them.

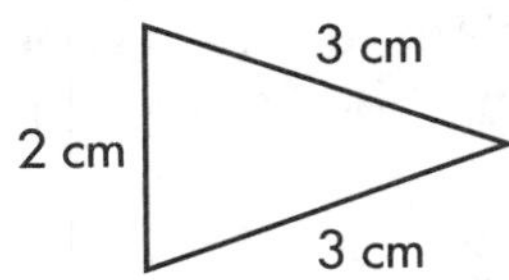

$P = s + s + s = 2 + 3 + 3$

$P = 8$ cm

When you know that certain sides are equal, you can calculate the missing sides.

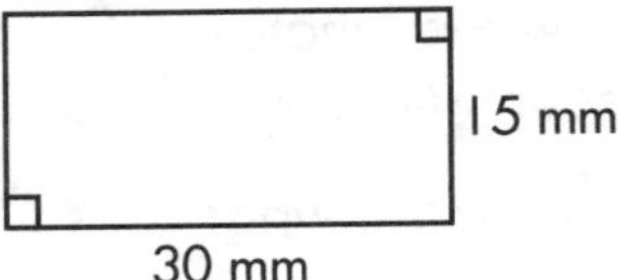

$P = 2l + 2w$ or $2(l + w)$

$P = 2(15 + 30)$

$P = 90$ mm

If a polygon is **regular** (all sides are equal), multiply the length of one side by the number of sides.

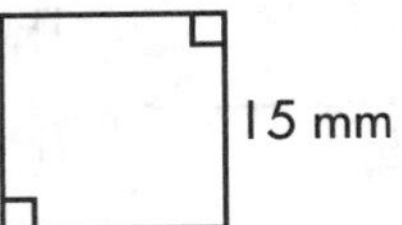

$P = 4s$

$P = 4 \times 15 = 60$ mm

Find the perimeter of each figure. Unless shown otherwise, assume each figure is regular.

	a	b	c
1.	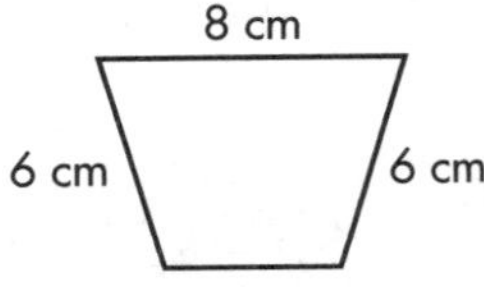 ________ cm	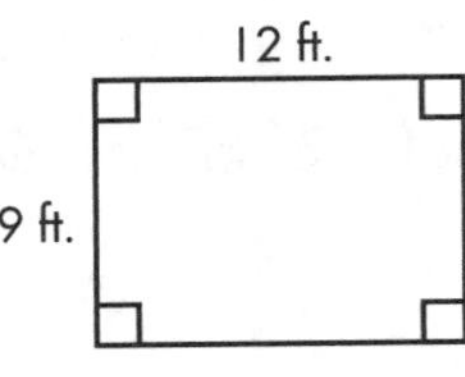 ________ ft.	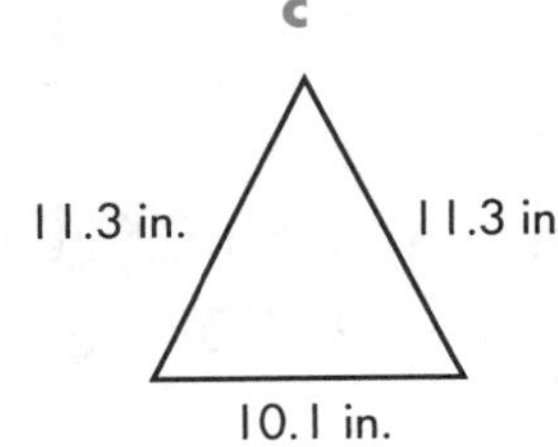 ________ in.
2.	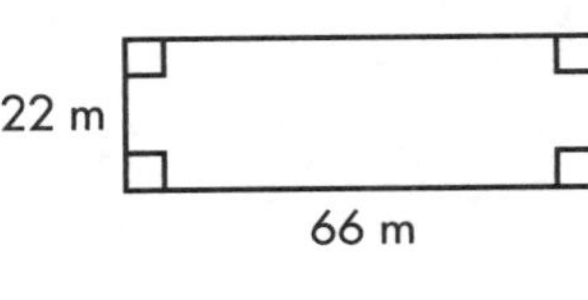 ________ m	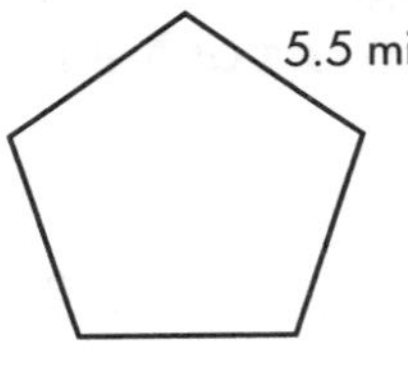 ________ mi.	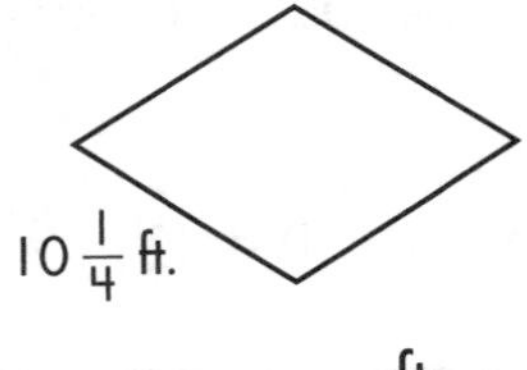 ________ ft.

3. On a baseball diamond, each base is 90 feet from the next base. If a player hits a home run, how many feet will the player run?
The player will run ________ feet.

4. Use the Pythagorean Theorem to find the distance from home plate to second base in the baseball diamond. Round to the nearest tenth
Second base is ________ feet from home plate.

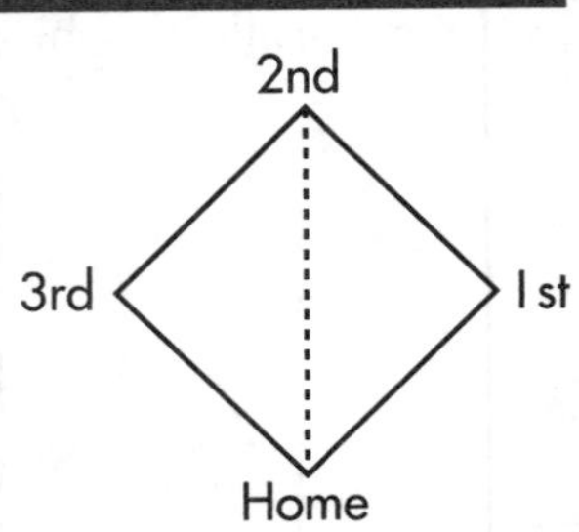

Lesson 9.9 Area of a Rectangle and a Triangle

The **area** of a figure is the number of square units inside that figure. Area is expressed in square units, or units^2.

The area of a rectangle is the product of its length and its width: $A = l \times w$.

5 cm

10 cm

$A = l \times w$
$A = 5 \times 10 = 50 \text{ cm}^2$

If you know the area of a rectangle and either its length or its width, you can determine the unknown measure.

$A = 24 \text{ m}^2$

6 m

$A = l \times w$
$24 = 6 \times w$
$\frac{24}{6} = \frac{6w}{6}$ $4 = w$
The width is 4 meters.

The area of a triangle is $\frac{1}{2}$ the product of its base and its height: $A = \frac{1}{2} \times b \times h$.

$b = 6$ in. $h = 8$ in. Find A.
$A = \frac{1}{2}\, b \times h$
$A = \frac{1}{2} \times 6 \times 8$
$A = 24 \text{ in.}^2$

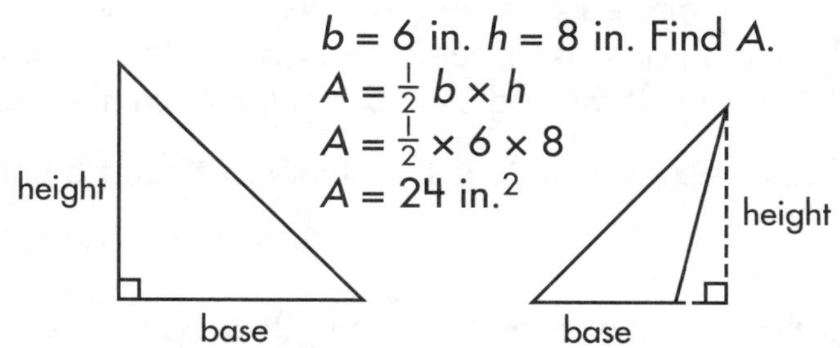

The height is the distance from the base to the highest point on the triangle, using a line perpendicular to the base.

Find the unknown measure.

	a	b	c
1.	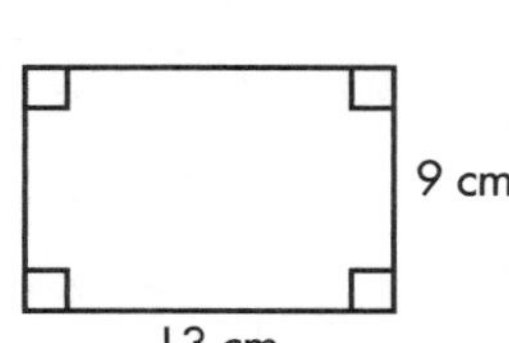 9 cm, 13 cm	$A = 126 \text{ ft.}^2$, 18 ft.	$A = 225 \text{ m}^2$
	area = ________ cm^2	width = ________ ft.	side = ________ m
2.	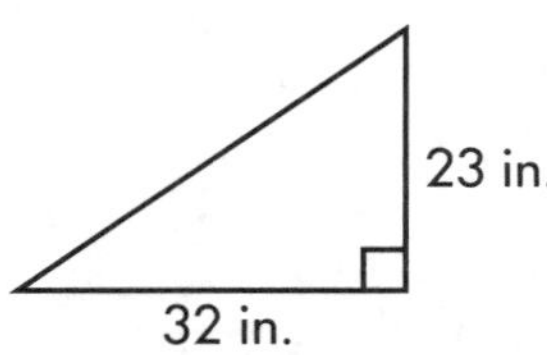 23 in., 32 in.	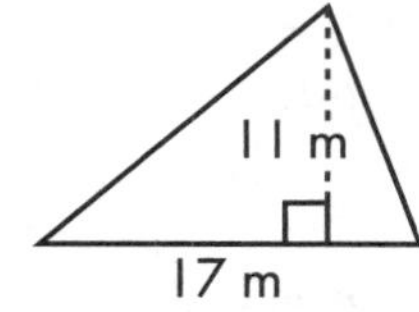 11 m, 17 m	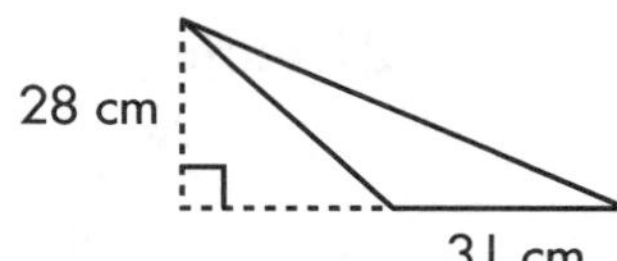 28 cm, 31 cm
	area = ________ in.^2	area = ________ m^2	area = ________ cm^2

3. Talia plans to cover a rectangular area of her yard with sod. The length of the area is 15 feet and the width is 12 feet. How many square feet of sod must Talia buy?

Talia must buy ________ square feet of sod.

NAME ______________________

Lesson 9.10 Circumference and Area of a Circle

All points on a circle are an equal distance from the center. The **radius** of a circle is the distance from its center to its outer edge. The **diameter** of a circle is the distance straight across the circle through the center. It is twice as long as the radius.

The **circumference** of a circle is the distance around the outside of the circle. The formula for the circumference is the diameter, or 2 times the radius, times π (pi), expressed as πd or $2\pi r$. The value of π is about 3.14 or $3\frac{1}{7}$. If the diameter is 4 cm, the circumference is 4π cm, or about 12.56 cm. If the radius is 5 cm, the circumference is $2\pi 5$ cm, or about 31.4 cm.

The **area** of a circle is the number of square units it contains. The formula is:

$$\text{Area} = \pi \times \text{radius} \times \text{radius or } A = \pi r^2$$

If the radius of a circle is 3 in., its area is $\pi \times 3 \times 3$, or about 28.26 in.^{2} If the diameter is 7 in., the radius is $\frac{1}{2}$ of 7 in., or 3.5 in. The area is $\pi \times 3.5 \times 3.5$ in., or about 38.465 in.^{2}

Complete the chart for each circle. Use 3.14 for π. Round to the nearest hundredth.

	a Radius	b Diameter	c Circumference	d Area
1.	7 m	________ m	________ m	________ m^2
2.	________ cm	11 cm	________ cm	________ cm^2
3.	________ ft.	4.8 ft.	________ ft.	________ ft.^{2}
4.	4.5 yd.	________ yd.	________ yd.	________ yd.^{2}
5.	21 mm	________ mm	________ mm	________ mm^2

6. Jay and Lisa baked a 12-inch (diameter) pizza. How big around is the pizza?

   The circumference is ________ inches.

7. Jay and Lisa plan to split the 12-inch pizza equally. How many square inches will each person get?

   Each person will get ________ square inches.

NAME ____________________

Check What You Learned

Algebra and Geometry

Use 3 letters to name angles in the figure at right.

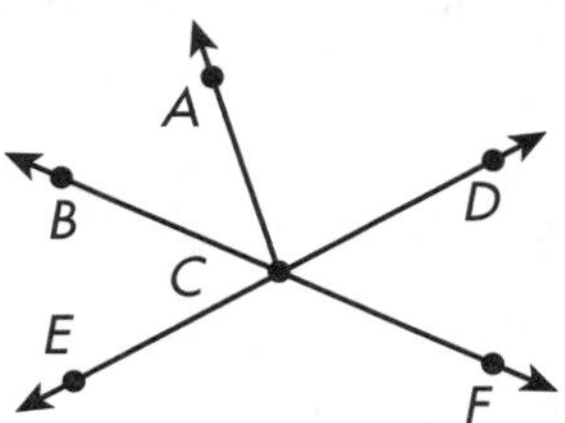

1. Identify the angle bisector. ________
2. What angle is adjacent to $\angle ACB$? $\angle$________
3. What angle is supplementary to $\angle ACB$? $\angle$________
4. What is the vertical angle to $\angle ECF$? $\angle$________

Label each triangle obtuse, right, or acute and scalene, isosceles, or equilateral.

5.

a

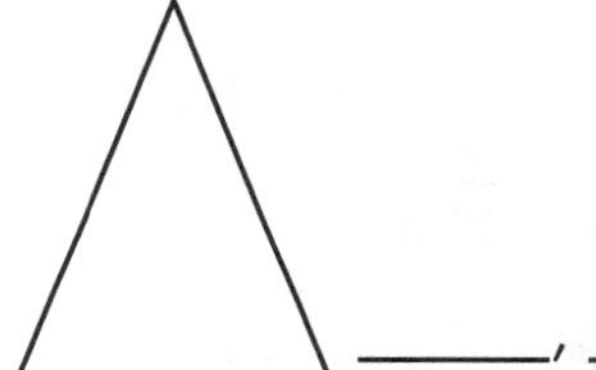

______, ______

b

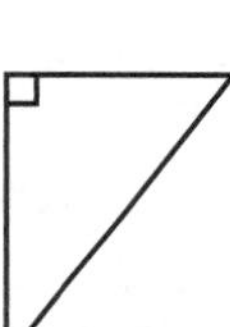

______, ______

c

______, ______

For these pairs of similar triangles, find the length of the missing sides.

6.

a

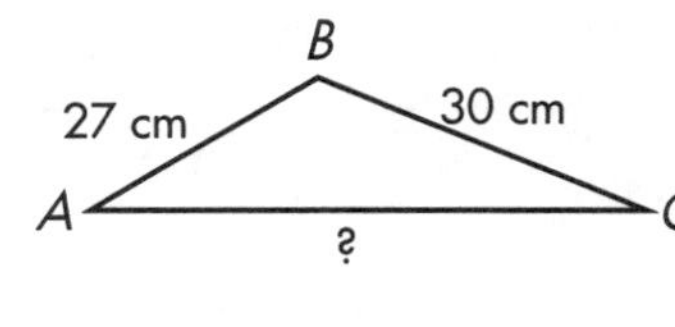

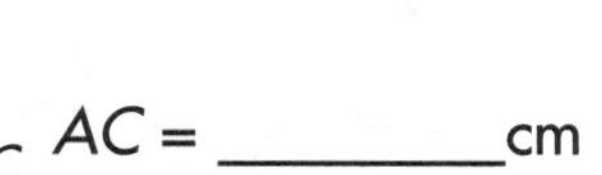

$AC =$ ________ cm

$DF =$ ________ cm

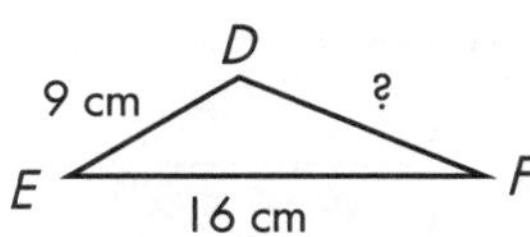

b

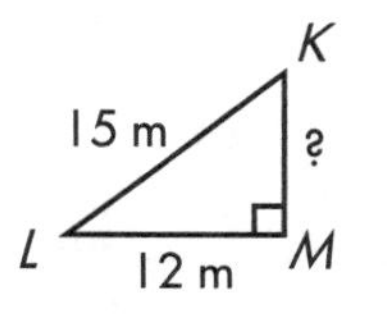

R
?
117 m
S
?
T

$KM =$ ________ m

$RS =$ ________ m

$ST =$ ________ m

7. A camper placed a 6-foot vertical pole for his tent. He attached a support rope from the top of the pole to the ground, 8 feet from the bottom of the pole. Write an equation to find the length of the rope. Then, solve the equation.

   Equation ________

   The rope is ________ feet long.

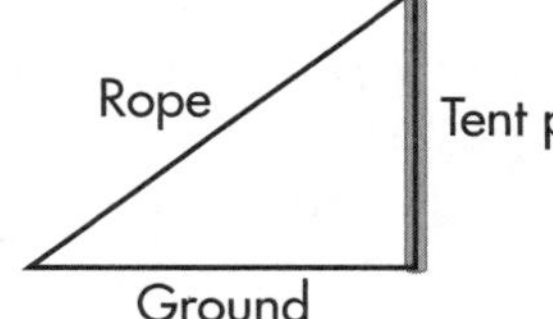

NAME ________________________________

Check What You Learned

Algebra and Geometry

Find the perimeter of each figure. Unless shown otherwise, assume the figure is regular.

8.

a

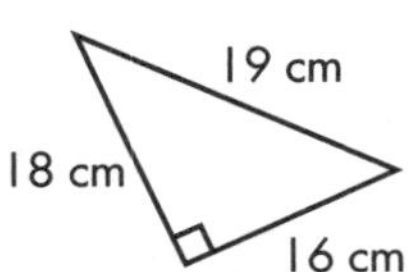

$P =$ ________ cm

b

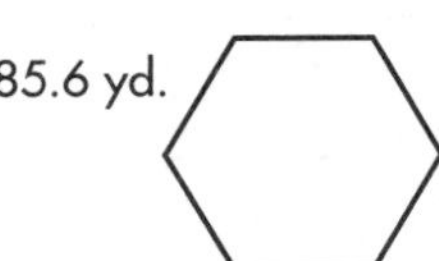

$P =$ ________ yd.

c

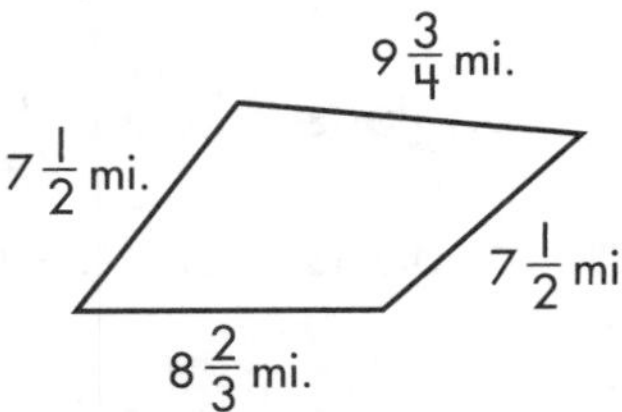

$P =$ ________ mi.

Find the unknown measure.

9.

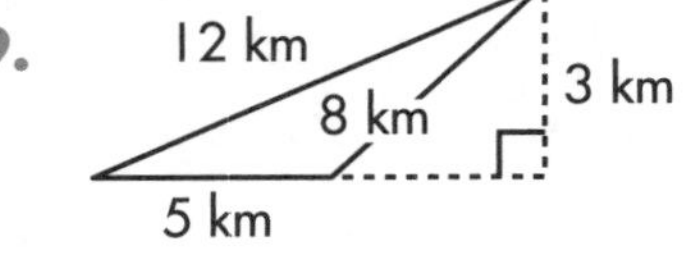

area = ________ km^2

5.5 m, 5.5 m, 2.3 m, 10.2 m

area = ________ m^2

$A = 294$ ft.^{2}

21 ft.

height = ________ ft.

Complete the chart for each circle. Use 3.14 for π. Round to the nearest hundredth

	a **Radius**	b **Diameter**	c **Circumference**	d **Area**
10.	22 km	________ km	________ km	________ km^2
11.	________ mi.	17 mi.	________ mi.	________ mi.^{2}

12. Tracy is sewing together squares of material to make a baby blanket. Each side of a square is 2 inches. How many squares does she need in order to make a blanket that is 24 inches wide and 36 inches long?

Tracy needs ________ squares of material.

13. $\angle XYC$ is similar to $\angle ABC$. How tall is the building?

The building is ________ feet tall.

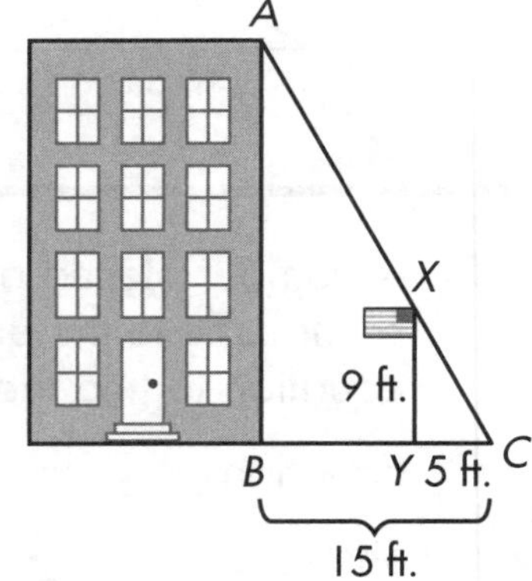

NAME ______________________

Final Test Chapters 1–9

Solve these problems. Write each answer in simplest form.

	a	b	c
1.	$\frac{2}{5} \div 6 =$ ________	$\frac{2}{3} \times 2\frac{1}{4} =$ ________	$4\frac{1}{8} - 3\frac{3}{4} =$ ________

2. Find the measures of central tendency in this data set: 40, 42, 38, 42, 39, 38, 42, 41.

   a. mean: ________ **b.** median: ________ **c.** mode: ________ **d.** range: ________

3. Runners finished a race in the following times (in minutes): 26, 30, 28, 34, 23, 36, 33, 28, 34, 24, 34, 36, 35, 31, 38, 27. Complete the frequency table below.

Points	Frequency	Cumulative Frequency	Relative Frequency	
			As Fraction	As Percent
20–24				%
25–29				%
30–34				%
35–39				%

4. How many runners finished the race in less than 30 minutes? ________

5. The greatest number of runners had times in which range? ________

This graph shows the change in the value of Dan's car over the time he owned it. Use this graph to answer the questions.

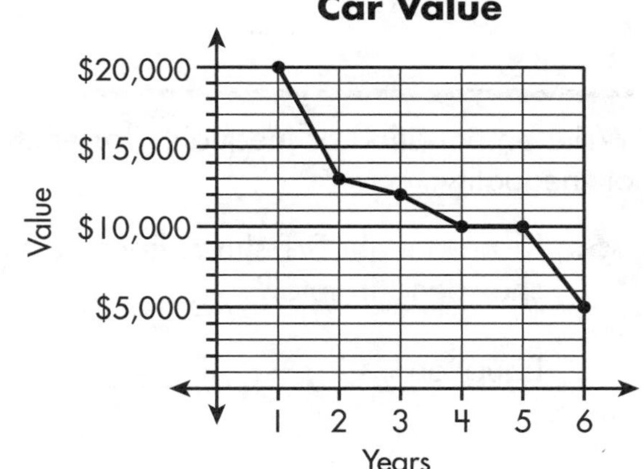

6. What was the value of Dan's car in Year 2?

   ____

7. In which 2 years did the car's value remain the same?

   years ________ and ________

8. Did the value of Dan's car increase or decrease over the 6 years? ________

   by how much? ________

NAME ____________________

Final Test Chapters 1–9

Solve the following equations. Write each answer in simplest form.

	a	b	c
9.	$-2.4n = 13.2$ ________	$\frac{p}{8} = 6$ ________	$18 = 2k - 4$ ________

Solve each equation. Write *null* or *all*, if appropriate.

	a	b
10.	$\frac{4w}{2} = w + 2$ ________	$6.4c - 8 = c + 13.6$ ________
11.	$3(6 + 2n) = 5(n + 7)$ ________	$24m + 4 = 4(1 + 6m)$ ________
12.	$2(p - 4) = 25 - p$ ________	$3(5 + 3y) = 9y - 11$ ________

Solve each inequality. Write the solution with the variable on the left side.

	a	b	c
13.	$8 + t < 26$ ________	$w - 18 \geq 45$ ________	$29 > y - 13$ ________
14.	$7h \leq 91$ ________	$\frac{c}{3} < -9$ ________	$-4p > 28$ ________
15.	$38 > 2n + 2$ ________	$-5d + 3 \geq 53$ ________	$5.25 < 3 - 5b$ ________

Write an equation or inequality for each problem. Use *n* as the variable. Then, solve the equation or inequality.

16. Kiara bought 3 T-shirts. Each cost \$15. She also paid a tax of 5% of the cost. How much did she spend in total?

Equation ________________ Kiara spent a total of \$________.

17. Raul set aside \$320 for workout classes at a gym. The membership costs \$250. He must pay \$5 for each class he attends. How many classes can he attend without going over his budget?

Inequality ________________ Solution: ________

NAME ______________________

Final Test Chapters 1–9

Complete the function table for each function. Then, graph the function.

18.

a

$y = \frac{x}{2} + 1$

x	y
−8	
−4	
0	
6	

b

$y = 2x - 4$

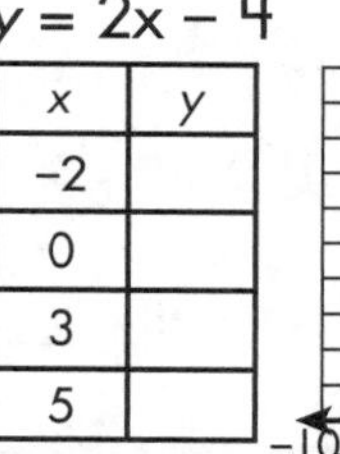

x	y
−2	
0	
3	
5	

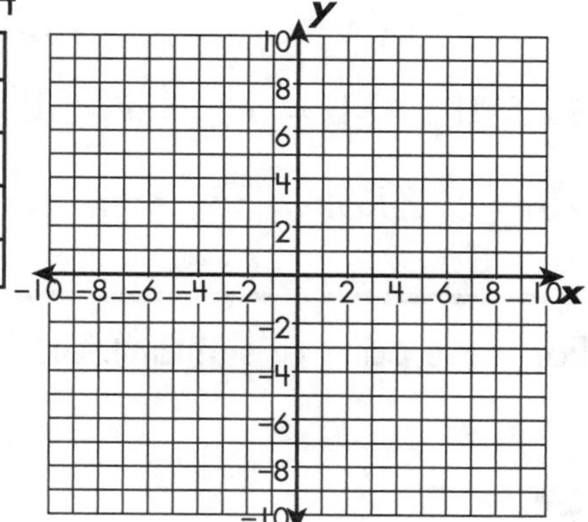

19. Maia walked 5.25 miles in 1.5 hours. Express her rate of speed as a direct variation equation. Use *d* for distance and *t* for time. ________

Write a linear equation for the information given below.

20. The slope is 8 and the line passes through point (4, −2). ________

21. The line passes through points (−4, 6) and (4, 14). ________

Create a scatterplot from the data below. Then, answer the questions that follow.

22. (0, 45), (1, 50), (2, 60), (3, 75), (4, 95)

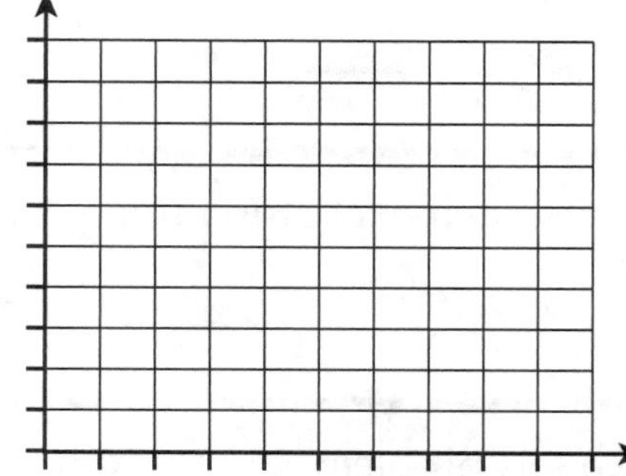

23. Is the relationship linear or nonlinear?

____

24. Is the correlation positive or negative?

____

25. If this data compares test scores (*x*) and the number of hours spent studying (*y*), complete the sentence below to describe the relationship between the 2 sets of data.

As the number of hours studied ________________, the test scores ________________.

NAME ______________________

Final Test Chapters 1–9

Answer the questions based on the graph.

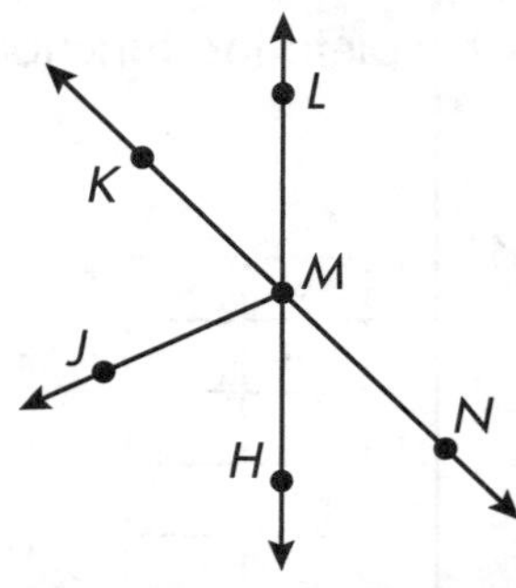

26. If $\overrightarrow{MJ}$ is an angle bisector and $\angle KMJ = 60°$, then $\angle HMJ =$ ________°.

27. If $\angle KMJ = 60°$, then $\angle JMN =$ ________°.

28. If $\angle KML = 35°$, then $\angle HMN =$ ________°.

For these pairs of similar triangles, find the length of the missing sides.

29.

a

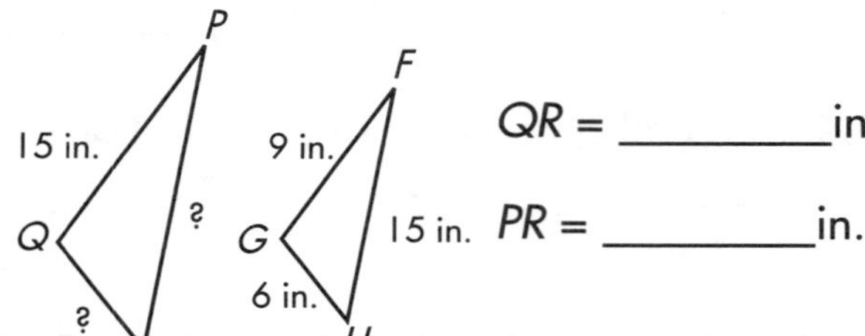

$QR =$ ________ in.

$PR =$ ________ in.

b

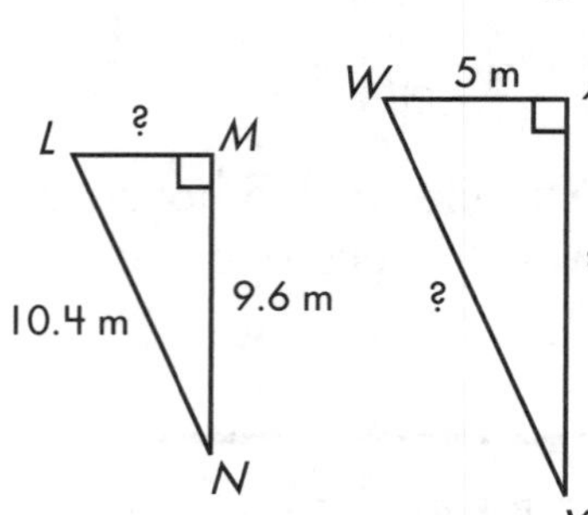

$LM =$ ________ m

$WY =$ ________ m

$XY =$ ________ m

Area of WXY = ________ m^2

Complete the chart for each circle. Use 3.14 for π. Round to the nearest hundredth

	a **Radius**	b **Diameter**	c **Circumference**	d **Area**
30.	4.2 in.	________ in.	________ in.	________ $in.^2$
31.	________ m	3.6 m	________ m	________ m^2

Rewrite each expression using a base and an exponent.

32. $3^5 \times 3^{-4} =$ ________ $8^{-6} \div 8^{-3} =$ ________ $2^6 \div 2^8 =$ ________ $4^2 \times 4^4 =$ ________

Solve this problem.

33. Jon has a photograph that measures 4 inches wide by 6 inches long. He asked a photo shop to reproduce the photo 25% larger. What will the new dimensions be?

New width: ________ in. New length: ________ in.

NAME ______________________________

Algebra Reference Chart

Number Properties	
Commutative Properties of Addition and Multiplication (L 1.2)	$a + b = b + a$ $a \times b = b \times a$
Associative Properties of Addition and Multiplication (L 1.2)	$(a + b) + c = a + (b + c)$ $(a \times b) \times c = a \times (b \times c)$
Identity Properties of Addition and Multiplication (L 1.2)	$a + 0 = a$ $a \times 1 = a$
Properties of Zero (L 1.2)	$a \times 0 = 0$ $\quad 0 \div a = 0$
Distributive Property (L2.3)	$a \times (b + c) = (a \times b) + (a \times c)$

Formulas	
Perimeter of a rectangle (L9.8)	$P = 2l + 2w$
Area of a rectangle (L9.9)	$A = lw$
Perimeter of a square (L9.8)	$P = 4s$
Perimeter of a triangle (L9.8)	$P = a + b + c$
Area of a triangle (L9.9)	$A = \frac{1}{2} bh$
Area of a circle (L9.10)	$A = \pi r^2$
Circumference of a circle (L9.10)	$C = 2\pi r$ ($\pi = 3.14$)

Pythagorean Theorem

$a^2 + b^2 = c^2$

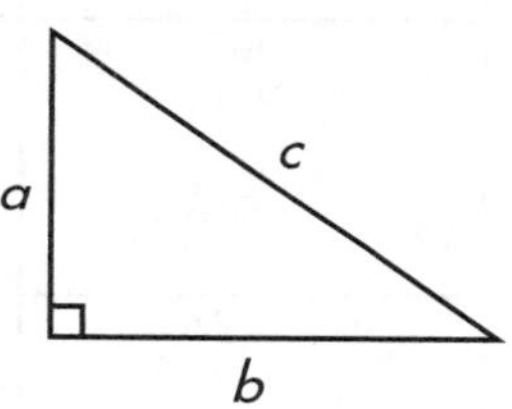

Triangles

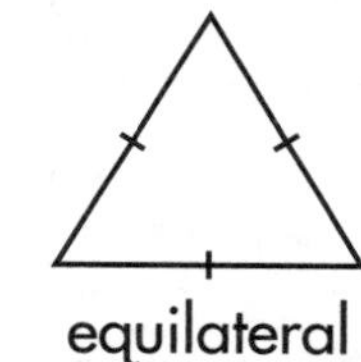
equilateral

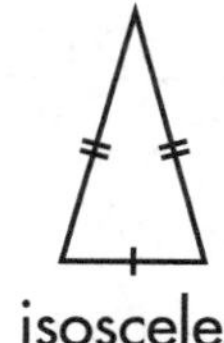
isosceles

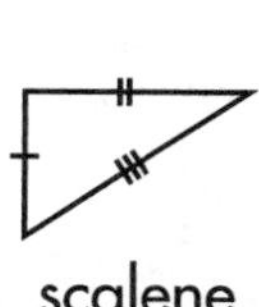
scalene

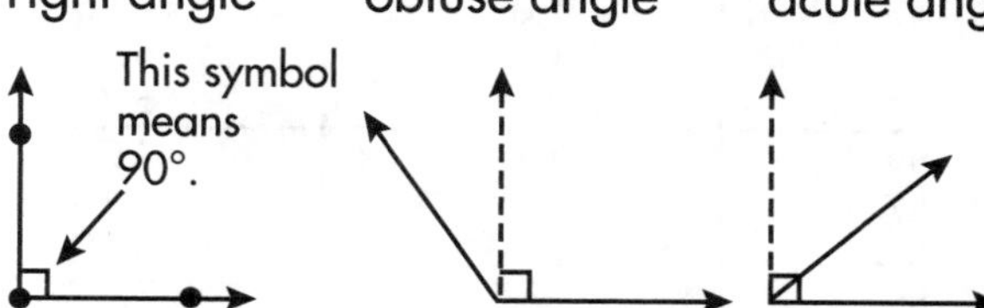

NAME ___________________________

Table of Squares and Square Roots

Except in the case of perfect squares, square roots shown on the chart are not exact.

Table of Squares and Square Roots

n	n^2	$\sqrt{n}$	n	n^2	$\sqrt{n}$
1	1	1	51	2,601	7.14
2	4	1.41	52	2,704	7.21
3	9	1.73	53	2,809	7.28
4	16	2	54	2,916	7.35
5	25	2.24	55	3,025	7.42
6	36	2.45	56	3,136	7.48
7	49	2.65	57	3,249	7.55
8	64	2.83	58	3,364	7.62
9	81	3	59	3,481	7.68
10	100	3.16	60	3,600	7.75
11	121	3.32	61	3,721	7.81
12	144	3.46	62	3,844	7.87
13	169	3.61	63	3,969	7.94
14	196	3.74	64	4,096	8
15	225	3.87	65	4,225	8.06
16	256	4	66	4,356	8.12
17	289	4.12	67	4,489	8.19
18	324	4.24	68	4,624	8.25
19	361	4.36	69	4,761	8.31
20	400	4.47	70	4,900	8.37
21	441	4.58	71	5,041	8.43
22	484	4.69	72	5,184	8.49
23	529	4.80	73	5,329	8.54
24	576	4.90	74	5,476	8.60
25	625	5	75	5,625	8.66
26	676	5.10	76	5,776	8.72
27	729	5.20	77	5,929	8.77
28	784	5.29	78	6,084	8.83
29	841	5.39	79	6,241	8.89
30	900	5.48	80	6,400	8.94
31	961	5.57	81	6,561	9
32	1,024	5.66	82	6,724	9.06
33	1,089	5.74	83	6,889	9.11
34	1,156	5.83	84	7,056	9.17
35	1,225	5.92	85	7,225	9.22
36	1,296	6	86	7,396	9.27
37	1,369	6.08	87	7,569	9.33
38	1,444	6.16	88	7,744	9.38
39	1,521	6.24	89	7,921	9.43
40	1,600	6.32	90	8,100	9.49
41	1,681	6.40	91	8,281	9.54
42	1,764	6.48	92	8,464	9.59
43	1,849	6.56	93	8,649	9.64
44	1,936	6.63	94	8,836	9.70
45	2,025	6.71	95	9,025	9.75
46	2,116	6.78	96	9,216	9.80
47	2,209	6.86	97	9,409	9.85
48	2,304	6.93	98	9,604	9.90
49	2,401	7	99	9,801	9.95
50	2,500	7.07	100	10,000	10

NAME ______________________ DATE ____________

Scoring Record for Posttests, Mid-Test, and Final Test

		Performance			
Chapter Posttest	Your Score	Excellent	Very Good	Fair	Needs Improvement
1	____ of 22	21–22	19–20	14–18	13 or fewer
2	____ of 20	20	17–19	13–16	12 or fewer
3	____ of 17	17	14–16	12–13	11 or fewer
4	____ of 15	15	12–14	10–11	9 or fewer
5	____ of 18	18	15–17	13–14	12 or fewer
6	____ of 16	16	13–15	11–12	10 or fewer
7	____ of 17	17	17	12-13	11 or fewer
8	____ of 15	15	12–14	10–11	9 or fewer
9	____ of 13	13	11–12	9–10	8 or fewer
Mid-Test	____ of 35	33–35	29–32	22–28	21 or fewer
Final Test	____ of 33	31–33	27–30	20–26	19 or fewer

Record your test score in the Your Score column. See where your score falls in the Performance columns. Your score is based on the total number of required responses. If your score is fair or needs improvement, review the chapter material.

Algebra Answers

Chapter 1

Check What You Know, page 1

	a	b
1.	expression	inequality
2.	equation	expression
3.	numerical	variable
4.	variable	numerical
5.	$x - 3$	$n \div 7$
6.	10×9	$a + 5$
7.	$3 \times n = 12$	$n - 5 = 7$
8.	$n + 2 < 10$	$18 \div n = 6$
9.	seven increased by *n*	Three times *n*, plus two, is twenty-nine.
10.	Property of Zero	Identity
11.	Commutative	Associative

Check What You Know, page 2

	a	b
12.	$8 + 9$	$(5 \times 3) \times 4$
13.	91	0
14.	$6 + 1$	3×4
15.	5×8	$12 \div 3$
16.	$22 - 2$	2×4
17.	49	13
18.	43	35
19.	5	15
20.	$A\ (-6, 2)$	$B\ (4, 5)$
21.	$C\ (6, -3)$	$D\ (-4, -3)$
22.		

Grid 1

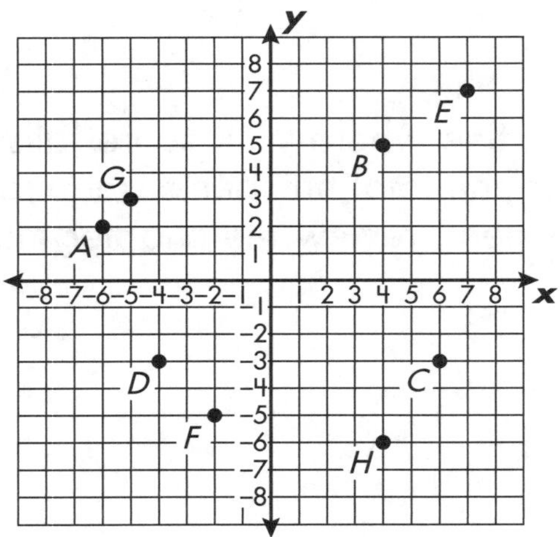

Lesson 1.1, page 3

	a	b	c
1.	variable	numerical	variable
2.	numerical	numerical	variable
3.	$x + 2$	$11 - 4$	
4.	9×8	$10 + r$	
5.	$b \div 5$	3×7	
6.	$s - 1$	$12 + 6$	

7. two more than *d*, or two added to *d*, or *d* increased by two, or a number increased by two
8. three times *n*, or three *n*s, or the product of three and *n*, or the product of three and a number

Lesson 1.2, page 4

	a	b
1.	Identity	Property of Zero
2.	Associative	Identity
3.	Commutative	Property of Zero
4.	y	$(6 \times 7) \times 8$
5.	$4 + 5$	0
6.	$(7 + b) + 9$	3×10

Lesson 1.3, page 5

	a	b
1.	equation	inequality
2.	inequality	equation
3.	$n - 7 = 5$	
4.	$9 \times 3 = 27$	
5.	$n + 5 < 60$	
6.	$10 \div n = 2$	

7. *x* divided by three is twelve, or a number divided by three is twelve.
8. The product of five and twenty-one is greater than one hundred.
9. Seven times *n*, plus three, is thirty-one; or seven times a number, plus three, is thirty-one.
10. Twenty-nine decreased by a number is less than ten.

Lesson 1.4, page 6

	a	b
1.	5×2	$10 \div 2$
2.	2×10	3×4
3.	$8 + 2$	$16 - 8$
4.	10×2	$11 - 8$
5.	10	2
6.	3	7
7.	45	19
8.	45	54
9.	11	36
10.	15	3

Algebra Answers

Lesson 1.5, page 7

1. *A* (2, 2); *B* (–2, –5)
2. *C* (–6, 4); *D* (3, –6)
3. *E* (–4, 2); *F* (6, 2)
4. *G* (–4, –3); *H* (4, –4)
5. *I* (–6, –5); *J* (5, 8)
6. **Grid 1**

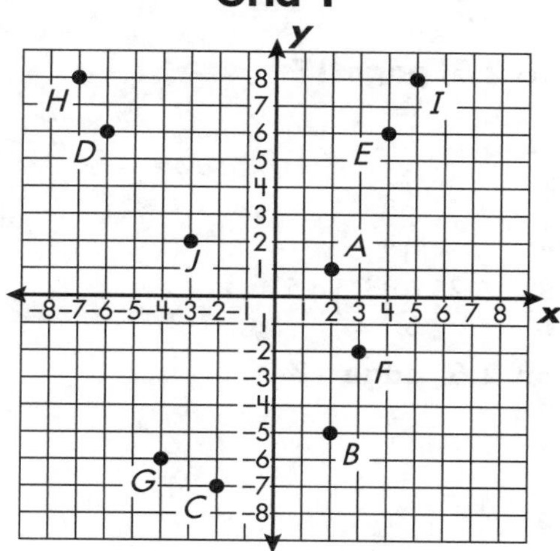

Lesson 1.5, page 8

1.

Tubs (*x* values)	Dollars (*y* values)
100	500
200	1,000
300	1,500
400	2,000

Profit from Cookie Dough Sales

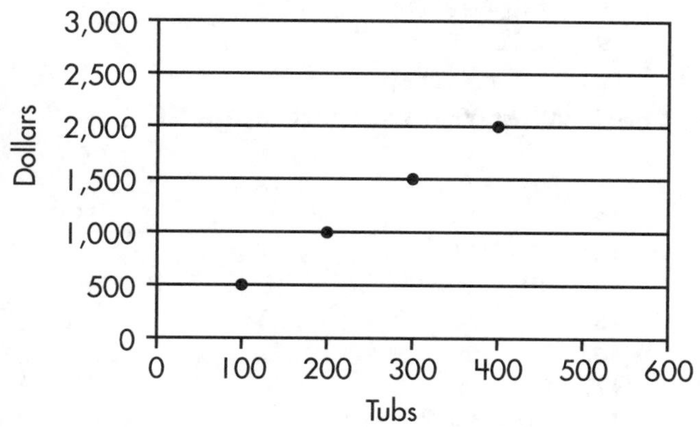

2. $2,000; 600

Check What You Learned, page 9

	a	b
1.	equation	expression
2.	expression	inequality
3.	variable	numerical
4.	numerical	variable
5.	$b \div 3$	$7 \times n$
6.	$42 - 10$	$7 - n$
7.	$7 - 3 = 4$	$12 \div n = 3$
8.	$x - 6 > 10$	$5b = 20$

9. *b* increased by twenty-two; Two times *b*, plus seven, is fifteen.

	a	b
10.	Identity	Commutative
11.	Associative	Commutative

Check What You Learned, page 10

	a	b
12.	0	88
13.	$(2 + 4) + 5$	8×6
14.	3×2	$4 + 3$
15.	$12 \div 3$	$37 - 4$
16.	3×2	$5 - 3$
17.	14	8
18.	11	3
19.	18	15
20.	*A* (6, 4)	*B* (–3, 1)
21.	*C* (–6, –6)	*D* (3, –5)

22. **Grid 1**

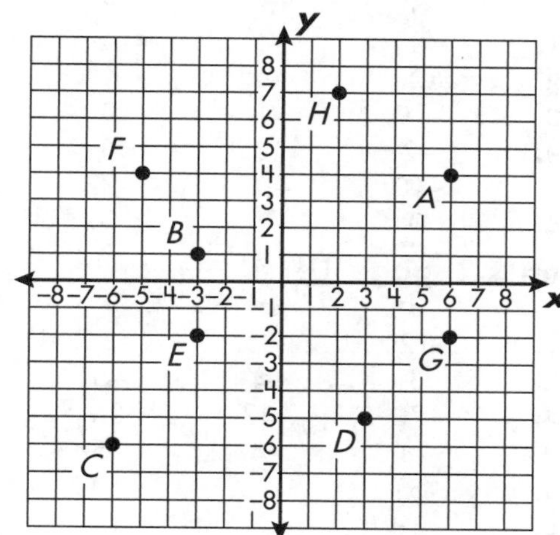

Algebra Answers

Chapter 2

Check What You Know, page 11

	a	b	c	d
1.	8	–8	2	–2
2.	2	–8	8	–2
3.	12	–12	–12	12
4.	3	–3	–3	3
5.	–5	5	–1	1

6. (4 × 6) + (4 × 7) 2 × (3 + 5)
7. (6 × 4) – (6 × 3) 4 × (8 – 9)
8. $22a + 18$
9. $-23b + 66$
10. $22c - 14$

Check What You Know, page 12

	a	b	c
11.	7	12	4
12.	23	55	46
13.	19	5	11
14.	9	9	7
15.	20	4	51
16.	5	27	0
17.	2	3	40

18. $21 = 9 + x$; 12
19. $160 = 8x$; 20
20. $28 = 10 + 3x$; 6

Lesson 2.1, page 13

	a	b	c	d
1.	6	–6	–2	2
2.	2	–6	6	–2
3.	–10	0	0	10
4.	–2	–6	6	2
5.	–10	–10	–22	10
6.	0	–7	0	–14

Lesson 2.2, page 14

	a	b	c	d
1.	12	–35	–36	20
2.	3	–4	–5	–3
3.	–72	–42	36	–50
4.	–8	–4	–5	4
5.	–51	7	–108	72
6.	–18	–7	11	2
7.	54	–49	38	–9
8.	–3	–21	14	–7

Lesson 2.3, page 15

	a	b
1.	(5 × 3) + (5 × 4)	3 × (4 + 6)
2.	(15 × 7) – (15 × 4)	5 × (6 – 7)
3.	(11 × 5) + (11 × b)	$13m - 13n$

4. $9a + 32$
5. $b + 12$

Lesson 2.4, page 16

	a	b	c
1.	5	8	11
2.	19	31	10
3.	34	101	13
4.	12	18	6

5. $6 = 2 + 1 + x$; 3
6. $15 = x - 3$; 18

Lesson 2.5, page 17

	a	b	c
1.	3	3	5
2.	22	7	26
3.	20	0	7
4.	12	9	30

5. $6.25 = 1.25x$; 5
6. $12 = 3x$; 4

Lesson 2.6, page 18

	a	b	c
1.	3	16	3
2.	12	9	4
3.	5	5	11

4. $9 = \frac{x}{2} + 4$; 10
5. $9 = 2x + x + 3$; 2

Check What You Learned, page 19

	a	b	c	d
1.	24	–24	2	–2
2.	–4	–14	14	4
3.	24	–24	–24	24
4.	3	–3	–3	3
5.	–6	6	–1	1

6. (7 × 2) + (7 × 3) 5 × (6 + 8)
7. (3 × 6) – (3 × 2) 9 × (3 – 4)
8. $23a + 18$
9. $-21b + 84$
10. $17c + 2$

Check What You Learned, page 20

	a	b	c
11.	8	18	4
12.	13	31	59
13.	11	–7	11
14.	8	6	12
15.	30	9	52
16.	5	28	0
17.	5	4	12

18. $10 = 3 + 2 + x$; 5
19. $33 = 3x$; 11
20. $5x = 20 - 7.50$; 2.50

Algebra Answers

Chapter 3

Check What You Know, page 21

	a	b	c
1.	3	9	14
2.	2, 2, 13	2, 7, 7	2, 2, 3, 3, 3
3.	11^2	6^3	c^4
4.	r^5	39^1	4^6
5.	1,000,000	144	43
6.	125	1	81
7.	4.2×10^{-3}	4.2×10^2	4.2×10^4
8.	72,5000	725	0.0725

Check What You Know, page 22

	a	b	c
9.	89	100	32
10.	625	24	9
11.	$\frac{2}{3}$	$\frac{3}{8}$	
12.	$\frac{5}{8}$	OK	
13.	$\frac{b}{a}$	$\frac{1}{2}x$	
14.	OK	$10c$	
15.	7^7	9^2	
16.	5^{-13}	6^7	
17.	$1{,}000 \times 1.02^{10}$		

Lesson 3.1, page 23

1. 9 = 1, 3, 9; 15 = 1, 3, 5, 15; Common = 1, 3; GCF = 3

2. 30 = 1, 2, 3, 5, 6, 10, 15, 30; 48 = 1, 2, 3, 4, 6, 8, 12, 16, 24, 48; Common = 1, 2, 3, 6; GCF = 6

3a. 2, 3, 3, 3 **3b.** 2, 2, 2, 2, 5

4a. 2, 2, 2, 3, 3 **4b.** 2, 2, 3, 5

Lesson 3.2, page 24

	a	b	c
1.	5^3	3^6	b^4
2.	23^1	n^5	12^2
3.	27	121	1
4.	625	100,000	55

5a. 17 **5b.** 36 **5c.** 64 **5d.** 2

6a. 87 **6b.** 64 **6c.** 22 **6d.** 1

Lesson 3.3, page 25

	a	b
1.	$\frac{3}{7}$	$\frac{2}{3}$
2.	$\frac{7}{8}$	$\frac{3}{5}$
3.	OK	$\frac{3}{5}$
4.	$\frac{1}{9}$	$\frac{3}{5}$
5.	$\frac{2}{3}$	OK
6.	$\frac{1}{2x}$	$\frac{2}{3y}$
7.	$\frac{1}{c}$	$\frac{4}{5ab}$
8.	$\frac{5n}{11}$	$\frac{7c}{13ab}$
9.	OK	$\frac{2r}{5}$
10.	$\frac{b}{10}$	$\frac{2pq}{9}$

Lesson 3.4, page 26

	a	b
1.	4^5	7^5
2.	8^2	4^4
3.	3^8	6^4
4.	9^3	8^6
5.	5^2	12^4
6.	5^4	10^7
7.	2^8	3^5
8.	11^3	2^2
9.	3000×1.02^{10}	
10.	1.02^5	

Lesson 3.5, page 27

	a	b
1.	10^{-16}	9^8
2.	2^{-1}	6^{-9}
3.	3^{-5}	2^{-8}
4.	5^{-9}	7^1
5.	12^{-6}	8^9
6.	6^{-2}	11^{-7}
7.	2^{-1}	7^5
8.	4^2	12^{-10}
9.	2.5×10^{-1}	
10.	10	

Lesson 3.6, page 28

	a	b	c
1.	3.84×10	6.21×10^3	3.1×10^{-2}
2.	4.7165×10^4	7.6×10^{-4}	3.6732×10^2
3.	7.95×10^{-1}	9.215×10^2	6.1321×10^4
4.	0.0000417	2,070	0.000936
5.	955	0.0626	81,300
6.	0.576	757,000	0.0037
7.	3.844×10^5		
8.	1.5×10^8		

Algebra Answers

Check What You Learned, page 29

	a	b	c
1.	7	3	4
2.	2, 2, 2, 2, 3	2, 3, 7	2, 2, 2, 3, 5
3.	15^2	5^6	9^4
4.	17^1	$s3$	q^5
5.	64	169	23
6.	64	1	10,000
7.	2.7×10^{-3}	2.7×10	2.7×10^3
8.	61,400	0.0614	0.000614

Check What You Learned, page 30

	a	b	c
9.	141	144	22
10.	32	990	6
11.	$\frac{5}{9}$	$\frac{1}{2}$	
12.	OK	$\frac{4}{7}$	
13.	OK	$\frac{2}{3n}$	
14.	$\frac{1}{12b}$	$\frac{1abc}{3}$	
15.	8^{15}	3^2	
16.	3^{-2}	11^{12}	
17.	$1{,}500 \times 1.03^5$		

Chapter 4

Check What You Know, page 31

	a	b	c	d
1.	0.8	0.35	0.112	
2	2.75	1.28	1.875	
3.	$13\frac{1}{2}$	$1\frac{5}{9}$	$6\frac{2}{5}$	$8\frac{3}{10}$
4.	$2\frac{2}{13}$	$13\frac{1}{3}$	$\frac{15}{8}$	$\frac{29}{10}$
5.	$\frac{15}{4}$	$\frac{21}{5}$	$\frac{17}{3}$	$\frac{32}{5}$
6.	$1\frac{1}{24}$	$1\frac{7}{44}$	$4\frac{1}{40}$	$7\frac{5}{42}$
7.	$\frac{1}{6}$	$\frac{3}{8}$	$5\frac{39}{70}$	$1\frac{1}{12}$

Check What You Know, page 32

	a	b	c
8.	$\frac{6}{25}$	$\frac{23}{24}$	$12\frac{23}{42}$
9.	$1\frac{3}{5}$	$13\frac{1}{2}$	$1\frac{13}{27}$
10.	4.5	15.3	$\frac{1}{14}$
11.	$\frac{1}{72}$	$-26\frac{2}{3}$	3
12.	15.5		
13.	972		
14.	$7\frac{7}{12}$		
15.	2,599.50		

Lesson 4.1, page 33

	a	b	c
1.	0.6	0.60	0.600
2.	5.2	0.15	0.096
3.	4.8	3.55	2.175
4.	$\frac{3}{4}$; 0.75		
5.	$1\frac{1}{4}$; 1.25		

Lesson 4.2, page 34

	a	b	c	d
1.	$11\frac{1}{2}$	$1\frac{8}{9}$	$5\frac{4}{5}$	$23\frac{2}{3}$
2.	$11\frac{1}{4}$	$9\frac{7}{15}$	$3\frac{1}{33}$	$7\frac{6}{7}$
3.	$\frac{13}{3}$	$\frac{49}{9}$	$\frac{14}{5}$	$\frac{23}{7}$
4.	$\frac{29}{4}$	$\frac{59}{6}$	$\frac{56}{9}$	$\frac{67}{8}$

Lesson 4.3, page 35

	a	b	c
1.	$\frac{6}{21}$	$\frac{5}{8}$	$\frac{2}{5}$
2.	$\frac{14}{15}$	$4\frac{11}{36}$	$11\frac{19}{42}$
3.	$\frac{1}{84}$	$\frac{2}{15}$	$1\frac{19}{56}$
4.	$2\frac{6}{7}$	$1\frac{7}{8}$	$\frac{3}{16}$
5.	10	$3\frac{1}{3}$	3
6.	$\frac{17}{32}$	$2\frac{13}{21}$	$2\frac{8}{65}$

Lesson 4.4, page 36

	a	b	c	d
1.	$1\frac{3}{20}$	$1\frac{23}{72}$	$1\frac{1}{2}$	$1\frac{7}{30}$
2.	$\frac{5}{9}$	$\frac{3}{10}$	$\frac{3}{20}$	$\frac{19}{80}$
3.	$4\frac{11}{12}$	$2\frac{13}{20}$	$3\frac{5}{8}$	$1\frac{29}{30}$
4.	$2\frac{13}{60}$	$2\frac{43}{120}$	$8\frac{1}{60}$	$7\frac{1}{12}$

Lesson 4.5, page 37

	a	b	c
1.	2.4	19.8	15.6
2.	$\frac{1}{2}$	6	$\frac{1}{6}$
3.	−2	−0.95	3
4.	$\frac{1}{45}$	$-11\frac{3}{7}$	2
5.	$1\frac{1}{8}$		
6.	6.5		

Lesson 4.6, page 38

1. 5; 26
2. 11; 44
3. 0.5; 7.5
4. $\frac{2}{3}$; $\frac{2}{3}$
5. 7.5; 40.5
6. 6; 15,552
7. 2; 31.25
8. 10; 10,000
9. 3; 607.5
10. 7; $\frac{1}{7}$

Algebra Answers

Check What You Learned, page 39

	a	b	c	d
1.	0.4	0.52	0.172	
2.	6.36	5.98	3.125	
3.	$12\frac{1}{2}$	$1\frac{4}{9}$	$10\frac{1}{5}$	$7\frac{1}{3}$
4.	$5\frac{5}{11}$	$4\frac{7}{10}$	$\frac{28}{3}$	$\frac{17}{2}$
5.	$\frac{37}{5}$	$\frac{47}{7}$	$\frac{45}{8}$	$\frac{41}{9}$
6.	$1\frac{16}{45}$	$1\frac{4}{21}$	$5\frac{5}{8}$	$6\frac{3}{10}$
7.	$\frac{3}{88}$	$\frac{1}{30}$	$9\frac{23}{28}$	$\frac{71}{72}$

Check What You Learned, page 40

	a	b	c
8.	$\frac{21}{32}$	$\frac{7}{30}$	$9\frac{3}{5}$
9.	$1\frac{7}{8}$	10	$\frac{17}{25}$
10.	4.3	17.7	$\frac{1}{16}$
11.	$\frac{1}{20}$	$-3\frac{3}{5}$	3.5
12.	19.5		
13.	$10\frac{1}{3}$		
14.	$5\frac{1}{12}$		
15.	12.31		

Chapter 5

Check What You Know, page 41

	a	b	c
1.	True		True
2.		True	
3.	5	24	5
4.	33	15	4
5.	$\frac{7}{100}$	45	$1\frac{7}{10}$
6.	440	$\frac{9}{200}$	28
7.	0.0312	23.4	0.72
8.	7.5	1.95	0.55

Check What You Know, page 42

	a	b
9.	42	50
10.	90	23
11.	4%	
12.	3 years	
13.	\$168; \$768	
14.	\$3,500; \$3,937.50	
15.	\$265.99; \$2,265.99	
16.	\$32.48; \$832.48	
17.	12	
18.	11.98	

Lesson 5.1, page 43

	a	b	c
1.	True		True
2.		True	
3.		True	True
4.	True		
5.	$\frac{3}{2}$		

Lesson 5.2, page 44

	a	b	c
1.	10	4	15
2.	7	10	75
3.	1	90	100
4.	1	7	11
5.	5		
6.	100		

Lesson 5.3, page 45

	a	b	c
1.	$\frac{1}{5}$	37.5	$1\frac{1}{5}$
2.	262.5	$\frac{41}{50}$	$\frac{57}{400}$
3.	$1\frac{16}{25}$	35	16
4.	95	$2\frac{12}{25}$	330
5.	0.0575	12.5	0.58
6.	115	0.09	3.5
7.	2.25	0.5	0.99
8.	80	382	0.5225

Lesson 5.4, page 46

	a	b
1.	18.75	12.5
2.	60	72.1
3.	200	440
4.	51	10
5.	22.50	
6.	20	

Lesson 5.5, page 47

1. 5%
2. $1\frac{1}{2}$ years
3. \$176
4. \$6,500
5. 675
6. 4,000

Lesson 5.6, page 48

1. \$3,401.22
2. \$3,522.72
3. \$1,607.79
4. \$735.66
5. \$541.21; \$550

Algebra Answers

Check What You Learned, page 49

	a	b	c
1.	True	True	
2.	True		True
3.	8	10	9
4.	15	10	1
5.	$\frac{9}{10}$	120	$\frac{7}{20}$
6.	95	$\frac{3}{25}$	48
7.	0.0607	43.5	0.59
8.	9.8	2.33	0.72

Check What You Learned, page 50

	a	b
9.	71.75	35
10.	55	52

11. 5%
12. 2 years
13. \$112.50; \$862.50
14. \$3000; \$3090
15. \$434.87; \$4434.87
16. \$84.93; \$584.93
17. 8
18. 5.85

Mid-Test, page 51

	a	b	c
1.	*p*	9 + (*k* + 3)	
2.	7*n* × *z*	6 (*w* + *x*)	
3.	8 ÷ –4; 7	(–6 + 3); –8	(2 + 6); –96
4.	15 ÷ 3; 16	(8 – 3); 1.25	(6 – 3); 132
5.	72	91	9
6.	4	39	11
7.	0	90	7

8. $8n = \$54$; \$6.75
9. $(2n - 3) + n = 33$; Jack: 12; Dion: 21

Mid-Test, page 52

	a	b	c
10.	(4, 8)	(–3, –8)	(–6, 6)

11–12.

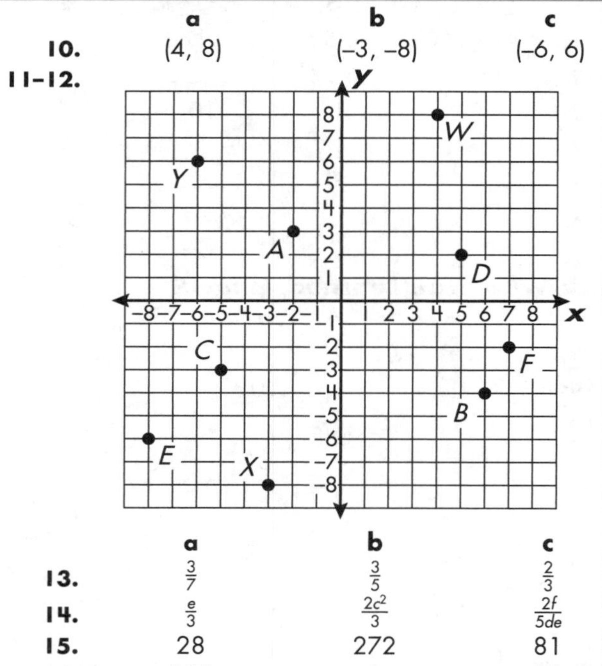

	a	b	c
13.	$\frac{3}{7}$	$\frac{3}{5}$	$\frac{2}{3}$
14.	$\frac{e}{3}$	$\frac{2c^2}{3}$	$\frac{2f}{5de}$
15.	28	272	81
16.	100	8	39
17.	7^{-3}	4^{-8}	6^{12}
18.	7.564×10^3	8.97×10^{-2}	3.2857×10

Mid-Test, page 53

	a	b	c
19.	$7\frac{7}{12}$	$4\frac{5}{8}$	$\frac{4}{9}$
20.	$1\frac{1}{4}$	10	$\frac{26}{63}$
21.	–1.7	$\frac{1}{8}$	3.875
22.	$-5\frac{1}{3}$	$\frac{1}{6}$	$-\frac{1}{6}$
23.	8.75	$\frac{1}{4}$	

24. $2\frac{1}{3} + \frac{3}{4} + 1\frac{1}{6} = n$; $4\frac{1}{4}$
25. $6\frac{1}{4} \div 1\frac{1}{4} = n$; 5

Mid-Test, page 54

	a	b	c
26.	$1\frac{7}{8}$	88	128
27.	$\frac{1}{2}$	6	35
28.	20	14.7	201.4
29.	84	20	20.5
30.	864		
31.	39		
32.	12.5		
33.	8		

34. \$749.18; \$6749.18
35. \$31.14; \$331.14

Algebra Answers

Chapter 6

Check What You Know, page 55

1. sleeping
2. 25%
3. 90
4. 6
5. Suki
6. Chloe, Dylan
7. 1
8. increased; 0.2
9. 10
10. 5
11. 6
12. 6
13. 12

Check What You Know, page 56

	a	b
14.	18	155
	19	153
	19	125
	10	74

15.

Height (in.)	Frequency	Cumulative Frequency	Relative Frequency	
			As Fraction	As Percent
58–59	6	6	$\frac{6}{31}$	19.4%
60–61	4	10	$\frac{4}{31}$	12.9%
62–63	5	15	$\frac{5}{31}$	16.1%
64–65	7	22	$\frac{7}{31}$	22.6%
66–67	3	25	$\frac{3}{31}$	9.7%
68–69	3	28	$\frac{3}{31}$	9.7%
70–71	2	30	$\frac{2}{31}$	6.5%
72–73	1	31	$\frac{1}{31}$	3.2%

16. 64–65
17. 3; 9.7%
18. $\frac{1}{3}$
19. $\frac{1}{2}$

Lesson 6.1, page 57

1. $\frac{1}{6}$
2. $\frac{1}{3}$
3. $\frac{1}{36}$
4. $\frac{1}{4}$
5. $\frac{1}{2}$

Lesson 6.2, page 58

1.

Temperature	Frequency	Cumulative Frequency	Relative Frequency	
			As Fraction	As Percent
35–40	2	2	$\frac{2}{31}$	6.5%
41–45	3	5	$\frac{3}{31}$	9.7%
46–50	6	11	$\frac{6}{31}$	19.4%
51–55	4	15	$\frac{4}{31}$	12.9%
56–60	4	19	$\frac{4}{31}$	12.9%
61–65	7	26	$\frac{7}{31}$	22.6%
66–70	3	29	$\frac{3}{31}$	9.7%
71–75	1	30	$\frac{1}{31}$	3.2%
76–80	1	31	$\frac{1}{31}$	3.2%

2. 2
3. 25.8%

Algebra Answers

Lesson 6.3, page 59

	a	b
1.	57	72
	60	71
	68	69
	27	15
2.	11.6	
	12	
	13	
	5	

Lesson 6.4, page 60

1. 4
2. 9
3. 21
4. 62
5. 52
6. 55.4
7. 38

Lesson 6.5, page 61

1. dance
2. 11
3. 55
4. 20
5. 61.25
6. 62.5
7. 65
8. mean

Lesson 6.6, page 62

1. paper
2. 31%
3. 77.5 million
4. 64.75 million
5. 28.6%
6. 12.4%
7. about 45
8. about 104 million

Check What You Learned, page 63

1. clothing
2. 25%
3. 90
4. $2
5. 1995; 1997
6. 287
7. 1998 and 1999; mode
8. 5
9. 6.5
10. 6.9

Check What You Learned, page 64

	a	b
11.	69.6	139.1
	69	139
	57	154
	39	39

12.

$ Raised	Frequency	Cumulative Frequency	Relative Frequency	
			As Fraction	As Percent
0–25	2	2	$\frac{1}{10}$	10%
26–50	5	7	$\frac{1}{4}$	25%
51–75	2	9	$\frac{1}{10}$	10%
76–100	4	13	$\frac{1}{5}$	20%
101–125	3	16	$\frac{3}{20}$	15%
126–150	1	17	$\frac{1}{20}$	5%
151–175	2	19	$\frac{1}{10}$	10%
176–200	1	20	$\frac{1}{20}$	5%

13. 7; 35%
14. $26–$50
15. $\frac{1}{13}$
16. $\frac{2}{13}$

Chapter 7

Check What You Know, page 65

	a	b
1.	15	$\frac{1}{2}$
2.	–1	2.5
3.	6	5
4.	7	all
5.	10	null

	a	b	c
6.	$>$	$<$	$<$
7.	$=$	$>$	$<$
8.	$\geq$		
9.	$\leq$		

Check What You Know, page 66

	a	b	c
10.	$n < 3$	$a > 22$	$p \geq 6$
11.	$w \geq -9$	$m > -3$	$x > 3$
12.	$b < 42$	$c \geq -3$	$k > -32$
13.	$y \geq 2$	$p > 10$	$n < 6$
14.	$r \geq 1$	$d \leq -7$	$x < 3$
15.	$y > 6$	$x \geq 5\%$	$k < -1.7$

16. $49.23 + *n* ≤ $200; *n* ≤ $150.77
17. $325.54 + *n* – $125.43 ≥ $300; *n* ≥ $99.89

Algebra Answers

Lesson 7.1, page 67

	a	b	c
1.	1	20	$\frac{1}{5}$
2.	$-\frac{3}{4}$	2	2
3.	–3	50	4
4.	7	9	7.1

5. $3x + 5 = 10 + x$; $2\frac{1}{2}$

6. $6 + \frac{x}{2} = 2x$; 4

Lesson 7.2, page 68

	a	b
1.	2	8
2.	all	–7
3.	4	null
4.	3	2
5.	all	$-\frac{1}{2}$
6.	null	1

Lesson 7.3, page 69

	a	b	c
1.	>	>	<
2.	>	<	<
3.	=	<	=
4.	<	>	>
5.	≥		
6.	≤		

Lesson 7.4, page 70

	a	b	c
1.	$x > 3$	$t < 15$	$m > 6$
2.	$y \leq 10$	$r \geq -4$	$n \leq 8$
3.	$p < -6$	$z < 20$	$w \geq -16$
4.	$x \geq 14$	$p \leq 31$	$y \leq 24$

5. $n + \$16.50 \leq \$25$; $n \leq \$8.50$

6. $n + 1.25 > 3.5$; $n > 2.25$

Lesson 7.5, page 71

	a	b	c
1.	$y < 3$	$k > 42$	$n \geq 3$
2.	$h < -4$	$m > -20$	$c \geq -12$
3.	$p < 2$	$n \geq 27$	$a > 10$
4.	$n < -1$	$b \leq -6$	$x > 16$

5. $\$6.25n \leq \$26$; $n \leq 4.16$

6. $4n \geq \$200$; $n \geq \$50$

Lesson 7.6, page 72

	a	b	c
1.	$p > 7$	$k \geq 5$	$x > -6$
2.	$z \geq 15$	$r < -10$	$b \geq -2$
3.	$n > 4$	$m \geq -9$	$w < 0.35$
4.	$y < 1.25$	$b \leq -13$	$a < -3\%$

5. $\$0.99n + \$14 \leq \$20$; $n \leq 6$

6. $\$8n - \$16 \geq \$200$; $n \geq 27$

Check What You Learned, page 73

	a	b
1.	3	0.7
2.	16	–9
3.	$\frac{1}{8}$	2
4.	0.7	all
5.	null	11

	a	b	c
6.	<	>	=
7.	>	<	<
8.	≥		
9.	≥		

Check What You Learned, page 74

	a	b	c
10.	$b < 27$	$k > 13$	$p > 16$
11.	$n \leq 5$	$y < 36$	$x \geq 3.5$
12.	$a < 7$	$c \leq -12$	$t \geq 22$
13.	$d > -3$	$g < 16$	$y < 3$
14.	$x \geq 2$	$n \geq 16$	$k < 4$
15.	$p > 0.1$	$a \leq 21\%$	$b < -2$

16. $\$0.85n \leq \$35$; $n \leq 41$

17. $1.25 + n \leq 4.5$; $n \leq 3.25$

Algebra Answers

Chapter 8

Check What You Know, page 75

1a.

x	y
−1	−5
0	−4
1	−3
2	−2

1b.

x	y
−1	−2
0	1
1	4
2	7

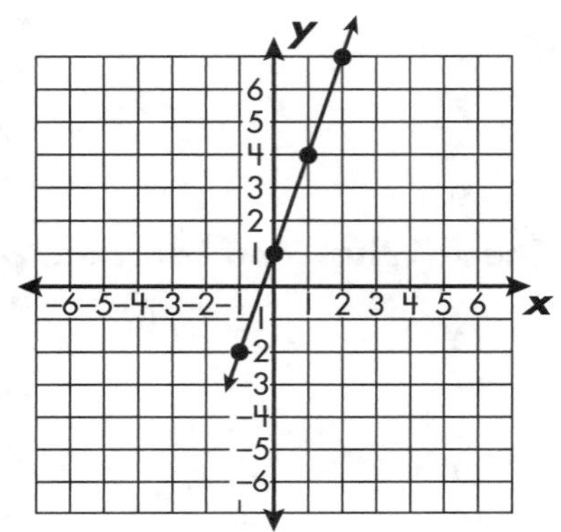

2a.

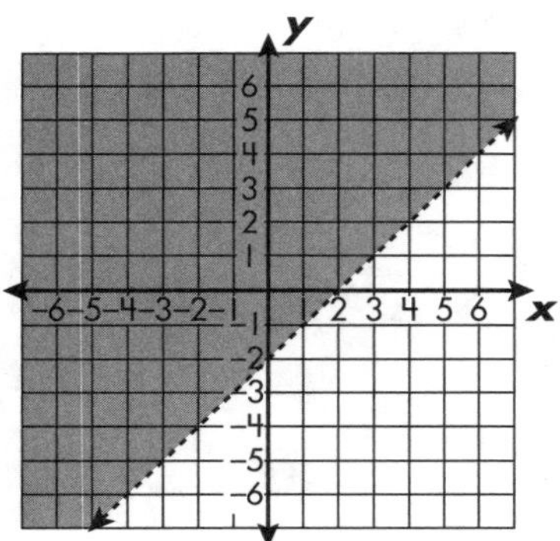

2b.

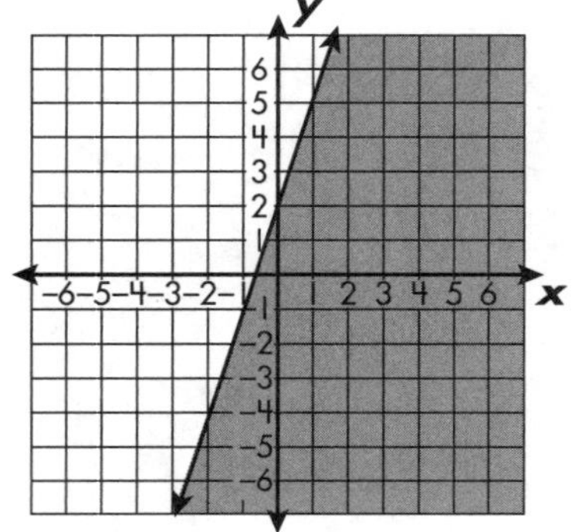

3. 6
4. 3
5. 40

Check What You Know, page 76

6. $d = 7.5t$
7. 45 minutes
8. $y = 3x + 2$
9. $y = 2x - 3$
10. $y = x + 5$
11. $y = 2x - 3$
12.

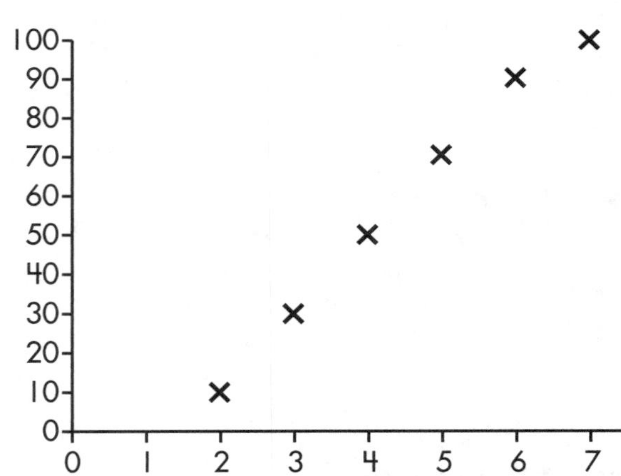

13. linear
14. positive
15. increases; increases

Algebra Answers

Lesson 8.1, page 77

1. a

x	y
0	–3
1	–2
2	–1
3	0
4	1
5	2

1. b

x	y
–2	–6
–1	–2
0	2
1	6
2	10
3	14

1. c

x	y
–3	–10
–2	–7
–1	–4
0	–1
1	2
2	5

2. a

x	y
–2	–1
0	0
2	1
4	2
6	3
8	4

2. b

x	y
–8	0
–4	1
0	2
4	3
8	4
12	5

2. c

x	y
–9	–4
–6	–3
–3	–2
0	–1
3	0
6	1

3. a

x	y
0	5
1	6
2	9
3	14
4	21
5	30

3. b

x	y
0	–1
1	1
2	7
3	17
4	31
5	49

3. c

x	y
–5	–2
–3	–1
–1	0
1	1
3	2
5	3

Lesson 8.2, page 78

1a.

x	y
–1	2
0	3
1	4
2	5

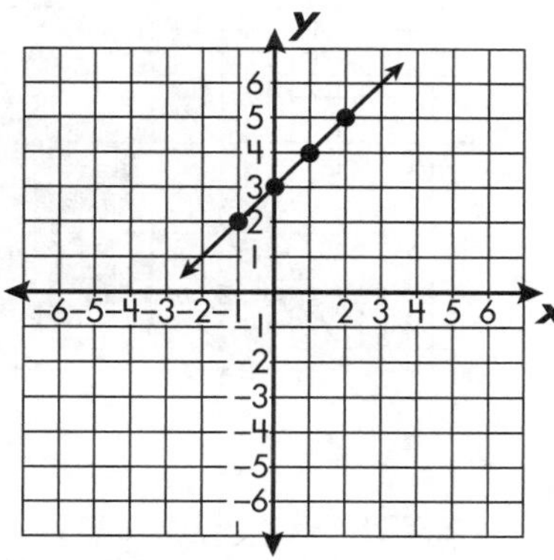

1b.

x	y
–1	–5
0	–1
1	3
2	7

2a.

x	y
–2	–2
0	–1
2	0
4	1

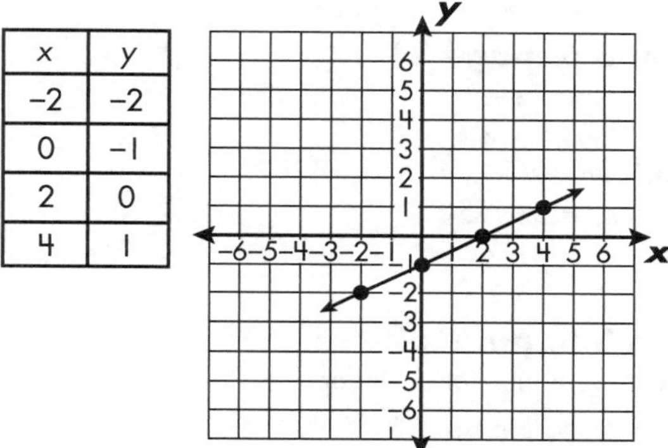

2b.

x	y
–3	–2
0	–1
3	0
6	1

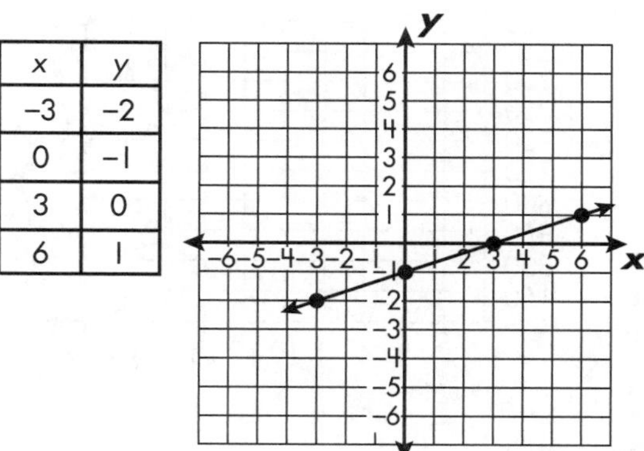

Lesson 8.3, page 79

	a	b	c
1.	2; 3	3; 2	1; –2

2. **a.** fixed cost
b. variable cost

Algebra Answers

Lesson 8.4, page 80

1. 7
2. 4
3. 15
4. $d = rt$
5. **a.** 200 (km/hour)
   b. $d = 200t$
   c.
   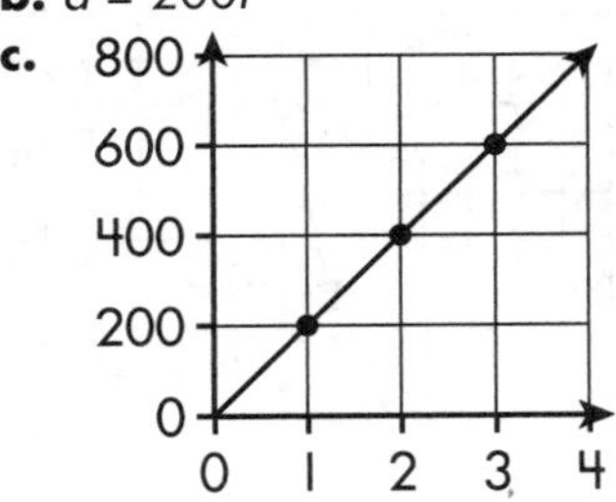

   d. $1\frac{1}{2}$

Lesson 8.5, page 81

1. $y = 2x + 1$
2. $y = x - 2$
3. $y = \frac{x}{2} + 6$
4. $y = 2x + 5$
5. $y = x - 7$
6. $y = 2x + 2$

Lesson 8.6, page 82

1. a. nonlinear b. linear

Lesson 8.6, page 83

2. a. positive b. negative
3. 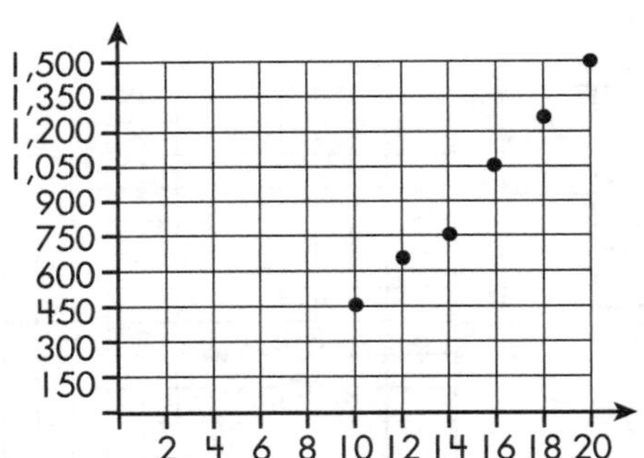

4. linear
5. positive
6. **a.** 6
   b. As the number of years of education increases, the weekly earnings increase.

Lesson 8.7, page 84

1. 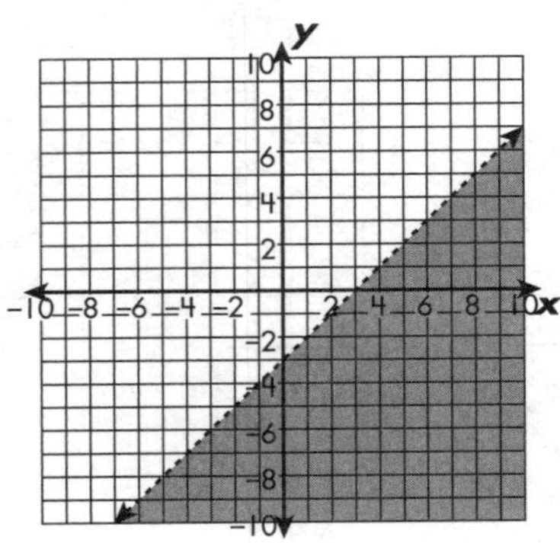
2. 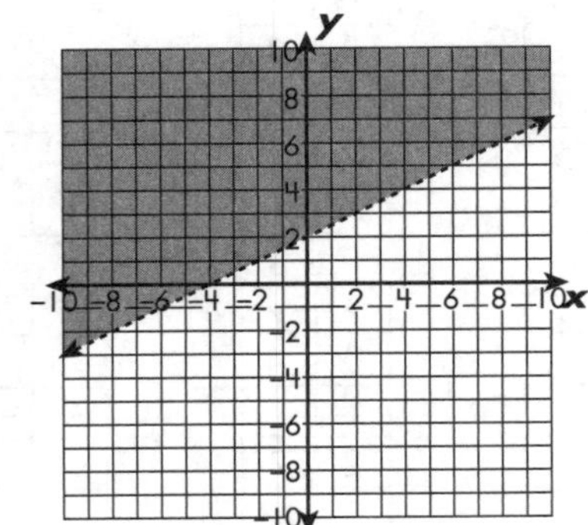
3. 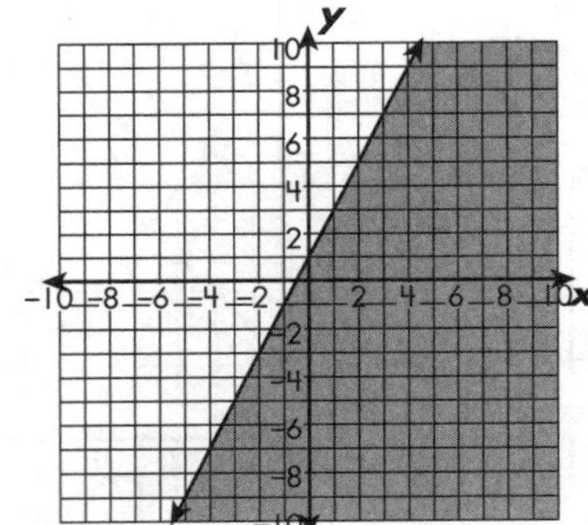
4. 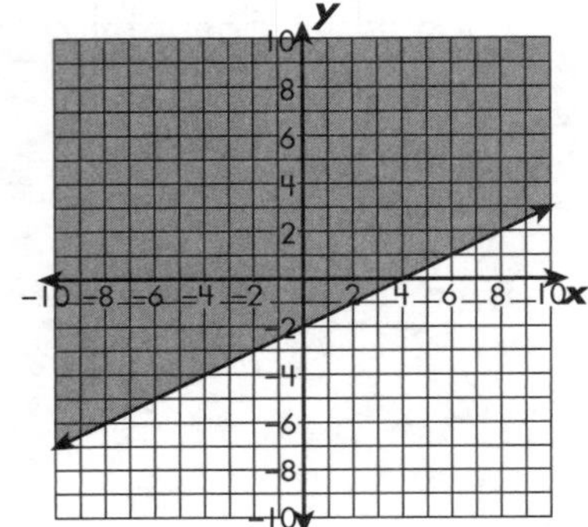

Algebra Answers

Check What You Learned, page 85

1a.

x	y
−1	3
0	4
1	5
2	6

1b.

x	y
−1	−6
0	−2
1	2
2	6

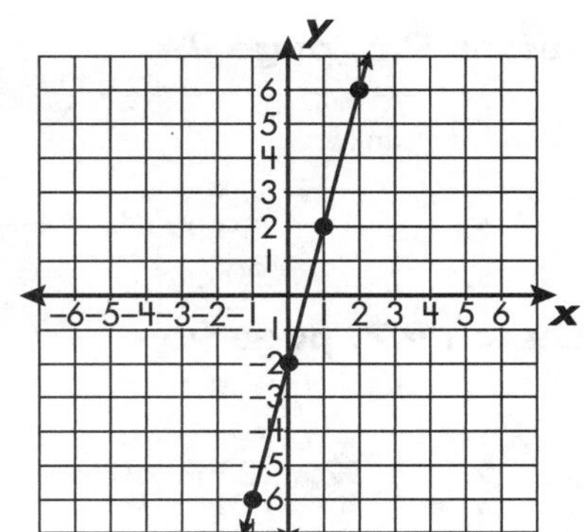

2a.

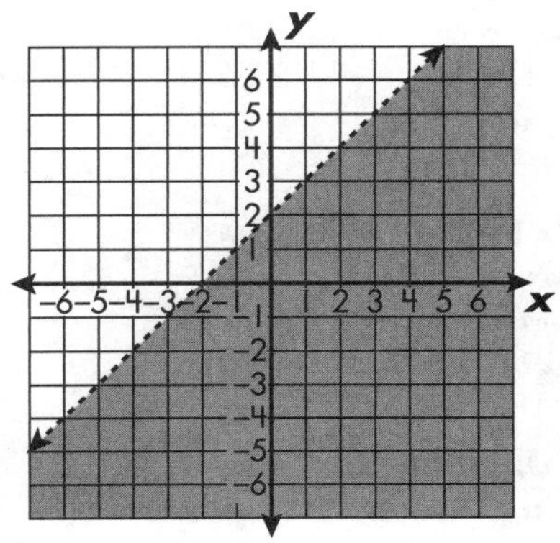

2b.

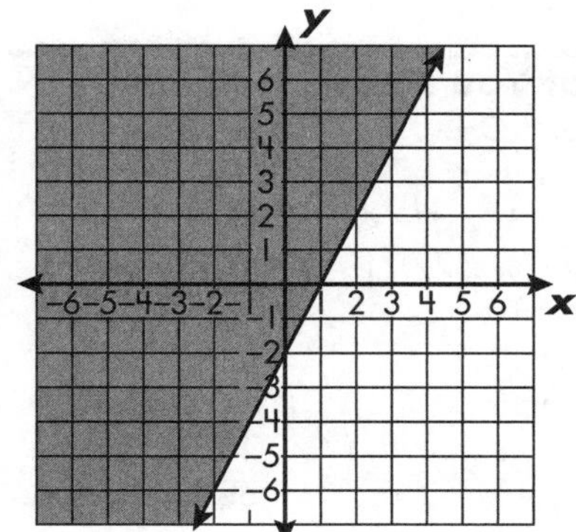

3. 8
4. 7
5. 24

Check What You Learned, page 86

6. $d = 16t$
7. $1\frac{1}{2}$ hours or 90 minutes
8. $y = 4x + 2$
9. $y = x + 4$
10. $y = x - 5$
11. $y = 2x + 4$
12.

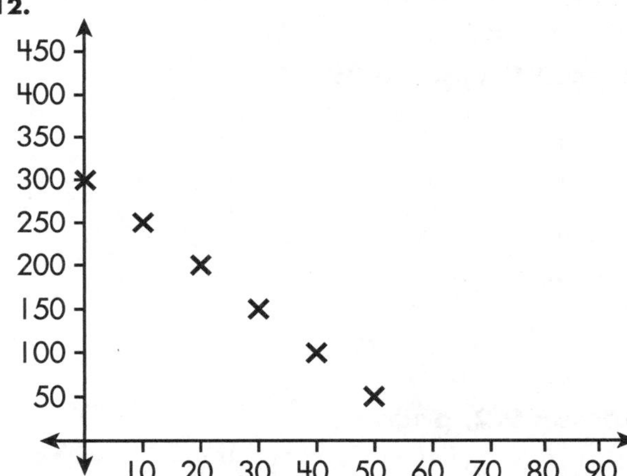

13. linear
14. negative
15. decreases; increases

Algebra Answers

Chapter 9

Check What You Know, page 87

1. *EF* and *GH*
2. *CD*
3. ∠5/∠3; ∠6/∠4
4. ∠8/∠2; ∠7/∠1
5. $\sqrt{100}$; 10
6. $\sqrt{125}$; 11.2
7. $\sqrt{380}$; 19.5

	a	b	c
8.	acute; equilateral isosceles	obtuse; scalene	right;
9.	$\frac{1}{5}$; $\frac{1}{5}$; $\frac{1}{5}$; yes		

Check What You Know, page 88

	a	b	c	d
10.	29.2 in.	28 cm	27 mi.	
11.	75 m^2	4.6 cm^2	12 ft.	
12.	8 m	16 m	50.24 m	200.96 m^2
13.	6 yd.	12 yd.	37.68 yd.	113.04 $yd.^2$
14.	a. 48 ft. b. 144 $ft.^2$			
15.	a. 13.19 m b. 13.85 m^2			

Lesson 9.1, page 89

	a	b	c
1.	3	9	6
2.	5	2	8
3.	1	4	10
4.	8; 9; 9		
5.	5; 6; 5		
6.	7; 8; 7		
7.	9; 10; 10		
8.	6; 7; 6		

Lesson 9.2, page 90

	a	b	c
1.	angle *XYZ*	line *EF*	angle *D* (vertex)
2.	point *C*	ray *AB*	line segment *MN*
3.	$\overline{XY}$; $\overline{YX}$	$\overrightarrow{QR}$	$\overleftrightarrow{DE}$; $\overleftrightarrow{ED}$
4.	∠*JKL*; ∠*LKJ*; ∠*K*	*P*	∠*G*

Lesson 9.3, page 91

	a	b	c
1.	100°; obtuse	50°; acute	90°; right

2. ∠*FEG* and ∠*IEG*
3. ∠*IEH*/∠*HEG*
4. $\overrightarrow{EH}$
5. ∠*DEF*/∠*IEH* or ∠*DEI*/∠*FEH*
6. ∠*DEI*/∠*IEH* or ∠*DEF*/∠*FEH* or ∠*DEG*/∠*GEH* or ∠*FEG*/∠*IEG*

Lesson 9.4, page 92

1. $\overleftrightarrow{WX}$ and $\overleftrightarrow{YZ}$
2. $\overleftrightarrow{PQ}$
3. Any 3 of these pairs: ∠2/∠4; ∠4/∠6; ∠6/∠8; ∠8/∠2; ∠1/∠7; ∠7/∠3; ∠3/∠5; ∠5/∠1
4. ∠1/∠2
5. ∠8/∠5
6. Any 2 of these pairs: ∠8/∠4; ∠6/∠2; ∠7/∠5; ∠1/∠3

Lesson 9.5, page 93

	a	b	c
1.	acute isosceles	right scalene	acute equilateral
2.	obtuse scalene	right isosceles	acute scalene

Lesson 9.6, page 94

1. $\frac{27}{36} = \frac{3}{4}$; $\frac{30}{40} = \frac{3}{4}$; $\frac{24}{32} = \frac{3}{4}$; similar

	a	b
2.	39 ft.	63 m
3.	90 cm	11 in.

Lesson 9.7, page 95

	a	b
1.	$\sqrt{296}$; 17.2	$\sqrt{672}$; 25.9
2.	52 m; 25 m; 60 m	
3.	24.5 km	

Lesson 9.8, page 96

	a	b	c
1.	24.6 cm	42 ft.	32.7 in.
2.	176 m	27.5 mi.	41 ft.
3.	360 ft.		
4.	127.3 ft.		

Lesson 9.9, page 97

	a	b	c
1.	117 cm^2	7 ft.	15 m
2.	368 $in.^2$	93.5 m^2	434 cm^2
3.	180 $ft.^2$		

Lesson 9.10, page 98

	a	b	c	d
1.	7 m	14 m	43.96 m	153.86 m^2
2.	5.5 cm	11 cm	34.54 cm	94.99 cm^2
3.	2.4 ft.	4.8 ft.	15.07 ft.	18.09 $ft.^2$
4.	4.5 yd.	9 yd.	28.26 yd.	63.59 $yd.^2$
5.	21 mm	42 mm	131.88 mm	1,384.74 mm^2
6.	37.68 in.			
7.	56.52 $in.^2$			

Algebra Answers

Check What You Learned, page 99

1. $\overrightarrow{CB}$
2. $\angle BCE$ or $\angle ACD$
3. $\angle ACF$
4. $\angle BCD$

	a	b	c
5.	acute, isosceles	right, scalene	obtuse, isosceles
6.	AC = 48 cm	KM = 9 m	
	DF = 10 cm	RS = 195 m	ST = 156 m

7. $8^2 \times 6^2 = c^2$; 10 ft.

Check What You Learned, page 100

	a	b	c	d
8.	53 cm	513.6 yd.	$33\frac{5}{12}$ mi.	
9.	7.5 km^2	11.73 m^2	14 ft.	
10.	22 km	44 km	138.16 km	1,519.76 km^2
11.	8.5 mi.	17 mi.	53.38 mi.	226.87 mi.^{2}
12.	216			
13.	27 ft.			

Final Test, page 101

	a	b	c	d
1.	$\frac{1}{15}$	$1\frac{1}{2}$	$\frac{3}{8}$	
2.	40.25	40.5	42	4

3.

Points	Frequency	Cumulative Frequency	Relative Frequency	
			As Fraction	As Percent
20–24	2	2	$\frac{1}{8}$	12.5%
25–29	4	6	$\frac{1}{4}$	25.0%
30–34	6	12	$\frac{3}{8}$	37.5%
35–39	4	16	$\frac{1}{4}$	25.0%

4. 6
5. 30–34
6. $13,000
7. years 4 and 5
8. decrease; $15,000

Final Test, page 102

	a	b	c
9.	–5.5	48	11
10.	2	4	
11.	17	all	
12.	11	null	
13.	$t < 18$	$w \geq 63$	$y < 42$
14.	$h \leq 13$	$c < -27$	$p < -7$
15.	$n < 18$	$d \leq -10$	$b < -0.45$

16. $\$15 \times 3 + 5\% (\$15 \times 3) = n$; $47.25
17. $\$250 + \$5n \leq \$320$; $n \leq 14$

Algebra Answers

Final Test, page 103

18a.

x	y
–8	–3
–4	–1
0	1
6	4

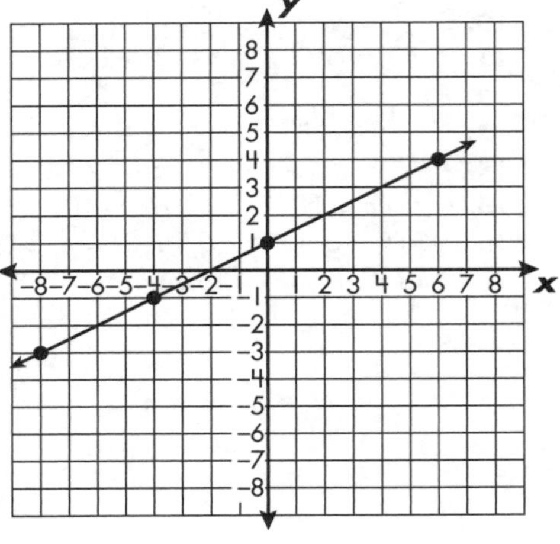

18b.

x	y
–2	–8
0	–4
3	2
5	6

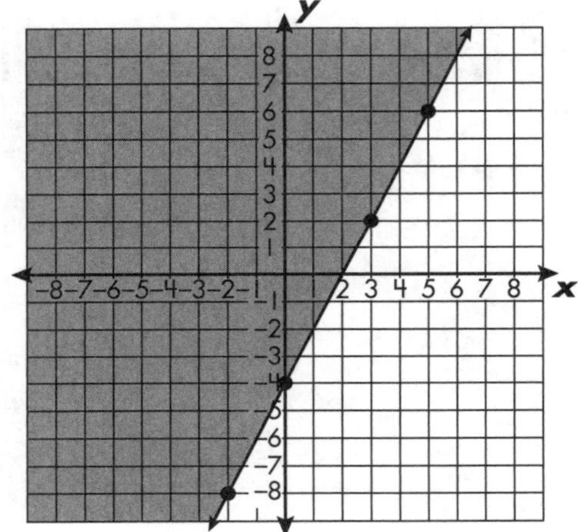

19. $d = 3.5t$
20. $y = 8x - 34$
21. $y = x + 10$
22.

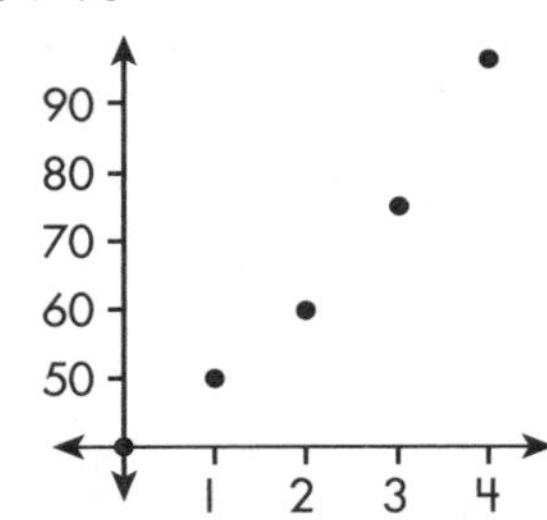

23. linear
24. positive
25. increases; increase

Final Test, page 104

26. 60°
27. 120°
28. 35°

	a	b
29.	QR = 10 in. PR = 25 in.	LM = 4 m WY = 13 m XY = 12 m Area of WXY = 30 m^2

	a	b	c	d
30.	4.2 in.	8.4 in.	26.38 in.	55.39 $in.^2$
31.	1.8 m	3.6 m	11.3 m	10.17 m^2
32.	3	8^{-3}	2^{-2}	4^6

33. 5 in.; 7.5 in.